T0128812

"For My thoughts are not your thoughts,
Nor are your ways My ways;"
says the Lord Isaiah 55:8

Are You Ready?

AMBER BARTLETT

WESTBOW
PRESS®
A DIVISION OF THOMAS NELSON
& ZONDERVAN

WestBow Press books may be ordered through booksellers or by contacting:

WestBow Press
A Division of Thomas Nelson & Zondervan
1663 Liberty Drive
Bloomington, IN 47403
www.westbowpress.com
1 (866) 928-1240

ISBN: 978-1-4908-1043-0 (sc)

Library of Congress Control Number: 2013917776

Print information available on the last page.

WestBow Press rev. date: 06/08/2018

Thanks be to God for growing me in my pain.
Thank you for my husband and
his time assisting me.

Special thanks to Bernise and Damien for your
giving spirits; without you I would still be
at my computer.

Introduction

What a beautiful day! Isn't any God given day supposed to be beautiful? Yes, but still I have my favorites. This favorite, however, goes beyond the day.... it's the entire month. It's October, and since I can remember, October has been my favorite month.

Today is just one of those almost perfect October days. The sun is shining brightly and the sky is so blue and every once is a while a cloud floats by. Not any cloud mind you; it's the cloud that is thick and puffy making you want to sit and float on it. Or reminds you of an oversized helping of whipped cream. All the trees are filled with brilliant colors and leaves are swirling to the ground announcing the changing of seasons. I'm sitting inside at the dining table safe from the chill of the morning air and the northern winds. I'm enjoying my morning alone with my puppy and two cats. I've got my cup of coffee and devotions taken care of. Now I'm just getting busy for the Lord as I sit here and type and listen to the crackling of the woodstove, the windchime blowing in the not so gentle breeze that was predicted on the evening news and the pounding of my heart.

I know that I should ignore the pounding heart and tightness in my chest. This typing task was appointed by our God so why should I feel this way. Well, lets see; because this isn't just any typing task it's something that will take awhile to accomplish and once it's completed they call this a "book". Really? (phrase of the past year) Yes! Really! Otherwise, there is no way on Gods green earth or any color for that matter that I would be writing a book! Never! Ever! In my lifetime have I ever said to myself…. "You know, I think I want to be an author". NEVER! It's just absolutely not something I ever desired to do. After all, my vocabulary is at the least limited I've never been a good reader and I type as slow as a snail.

I compare it to Esther going before the King, Moses leading his people out of Egypt and young David killing a giant. You know, we're just going through life like any normal person when you're called on by God to do something for Him. When the entire living of your life has prepared you to carry out a task for God and He has put you right where He wants you to be right when He needs you to continue to be a part of His plan. But if I've been part of His plan why does He need to "call on me" to further carry any of that plan out. It comes down to making a choice to be obedient, to walk your talk. Most of us Christians just glide through life hearing all these incredible stories how others have done something for God. When confronted, however, it becomes a different story. It becomes your story. It becomes your reality, your trial, your pain, your triumphant, your peace, your joy. Your life and all for Gods glory. Our lives belong to God and He will move you and use you where He sees fit and when you decide to follow Jesus you play by His "rules". Yikes! Sounds so controlling and restrictive and so not our kind of fun. I used to think that too before I decided to make the choice of following Jesus. However, now there is an understanding within myself that I've learned through church and Bible studies that God loves me and only wants the best for me. When I do things Gods way it gives me joy and peace within. I don't feel all bottled up and a life full of restrictions. I have a calmness and a freedom and that freedom is not just a feeling.

So why do I feel so much like Jonah? Jonah, Ezra, Moses, David? Who are all these people I keep referring to? They are all people of the Bible. They are the people that were called on by God to carry out His plan; to walk their talk of their proclaimed "faith". You can read all about them in the Old Testament part of the Bible, these are all the real life stories of things that happened before Jesus came to earth. Jonah is another guy that was called on by God. His choice was not to do as God was asking (obedience). Instead, he decides to jump on a ship and try to run from the responsibility that God was asking of him. So without spoiling the story for you Jonah ends up being put right back on the beach where God asked him to go to in the first place. You have to read that story, I'm telling you it is so sickening to even think Jonah had to experience what he did. The thing was though God needed Jonah to do something and there would be no running away. That is why I say I feel like a Jonah. God is asking me to do something that is totally out of my box. I don't write books, I mean come on!

So why don't I just "run away". I too, like Jonah, believe I have. It isn't the pack your bags and head for the door running away. It's been more like in my mind trying to come up with a hundred (to me) logical ways not to do this. It doesn't matter which way I try to twist this and just not take on this task it ALL comes back to one thing. This "thing" is a deep understanding that I know that God wants me to do this. When I think about not doing this "book" my entire body tenses up, I get a big knot in my throat, and the thought about what life will be if I do write the book never and I mean NEVER leaves my thoughts. Sometimes I pretend I'm just not doing it! You can't make me, You can't make me, NO YOU JUST CAN'T MAKE ME! Oh Boy! When I do that I have absolutely zero peace. I feel like a student being called down to the principles office or a child that has misbehaved and is waiting to discuss it when dad gets home; then you hear the car pulling up the driveway. There's just no escape from this. I thought it would be so much easier just to put it out of my mind and not do this "book". Continue on with life as I've known it. I believe with every ounce of my being that is not what God has planned.

My second and only other choice would be just to write this 'book'. Now you would think with that decision all would be a great peace and rainbows and angels singing. Not quite. It went more like this.

I'm sitting here typing and my chest is still tight, I'm deepening the eleven mark between my eyebrows and my arms ache from typing an hour. I've done my praying to God on this subject. All I can ask is for God to give me the words for this 'book', to send the message, for those He wants to read it do and to let Him know that I am not doing this for me. This is a work that I do for the Lord and He will use it for His purpose. It is my hope that you can know Jesus or further your relationship with Him if you already know Him. We all have a life that can be used for Jesus. This is part of mine.

Hello, I'm Talking to You

N ovember 10th, 2011. More time dated, marked in our manmade way. Our Bible teaches us that a thousand years is but a day to God, and a day a thousand years. I get that now.

Ever since October 1st, 2011, life has seemed like one long day. The lighted hours seem to go by too slowly, and the darkened hours pass too quickly. On top of all of that is just a big blur. Ask me what I did a week ago, and I would have to stop and actually make an effort to find the answer. Walking from one room to the next, I find myself wondering what I was doing in the room to begin with. Feeling normal one moment and crying the next. Wanting to eat everything in sight and feeling sick to my stomach. These, they say, are all the signs of a grieving person. They say grief never goes away; it only softens. Great! I will never be the same, changed forever, my life, because of the actions of another. I could point a finger at all the humanness of this, but I truly know that when it is all said and done, it is all God's plan. To think that I was living my life from one day to the next, being so pleased that for the first time in forever, my life actually seemed as if it was in order. We may believe we are the one in control of our lives, but we're not. God truly is.

I was minding my own business, going about daily chores and other routine seasonal preparedness, when I noticed something just wasn't quite right with myself. As usual, we have to put some label on our feelings, after all. I did, and I decided to label it anxious. Wait, though, doesn't the Bible teach us not to be anxious but to present our worries to God? Was I? I wasn't worried about anything in particular. I was just busy. I kept trying to have things done, anything from firewood to cleaning under my bed. I just wanted to tackle every project that I tend to put off. I chalked the feeling up to the stress of preparing for the winter season, ignored it by continuing on with my little cleaning projects.

It was noticeably odd to me that, on a beautiful sunny day, I wanted with every desire to clean off my desktop instead of finding something to do in the yard. That's how I operate here in Maine. When the sun shines, take advantage of getting things done outside, and on rainy or cold snowy days, do the inside stuff. Instead of doing the logical choice, I chose to go with the heart's desire. That was part of God's plan; I just didn't know it yet. In fact, that part of God's plan for that moment had actually started the day before.

The day before was a Wednesday. That morning, after the children had left for school, I sat with my second cup of coffee to read my two daily devotionals. I also like to review the devotional from the day before, but in doing so I was slightly confused. I thought I had picked up the same devotional and was reading it twice. That wasn't the case. What I came to realize was that both devotionals had titled the Tuesday lesson the same exact title! I pondered what the chances of that could be. Well, we know that with God, all things work for His glory, but for two people who may be total strangers to each other in different parts of the world and to have both their devotions end up on my dusty end table at the same moment in time for God to use to get my attention still just blows my mind.

So, there's me with these two devotions with the same exact title when the human brain kicks in. "Well, Amber, you know this probably doesn't mean a thing. After all, things happen in threes, and this is only two. I'm home all the time, so who else could possibly say this to me? I won't be speaking to anyone at any Bible studies or church services. I won't even be around an adult conversation until Sunday, anyway. Just put it out of your mind." So I did. On with my devotions and prayer time I went.

That desk, I've got to get to that desk.

Fine, I'd clean the desk. That's okay, though. I really did want to clean the desk. I know me. If I didn't clean the desk and decide to do something outside, I'd beat myself up about it until I needed to find or make the time to clean it. Who's to know when that would be? Besides, it had been quite some time since I had even wanted to dive right into that chore. So off I went.

I dug into various piles of paperwork that needed filing. I made the "keep it" pile and also had the trash basket right handy. What's this, save that, toss this, save that. I was actually enjoying watching the desktop coming more into view. Then, what's this? I picked up a piece of notepad paper, which I had saved with a phone number that belonged to who knows who. Above that, I had written a short phrase. About a year and a half ago, I had wanted to start a Christian t-shirt ministry, so when I heard or thought of a good catchphrase, I'd write it down and toss it in a drawer with the others. Well, this paper never reached that drawer. I read what I had written and was shocked. You've got to be kidding. I couldn't even believe this! It read the same exact words as the two devotionals the day before. It read, "ARE YOU READY?"

I couldn't believe it! I stopped what I was doing at that very moment. After all, this was the third time, and I've always lived with things happening in threes. I stopped what I was doing and stood up. I looked up toward the heavens and said out loud, "Okay, God, I don't know what you want me to be ready for. Ready for what? I don't know if I'm ready. Ready for what? How am I to know if I am ready for something when I have no idea what I should be ready for? You know what God? I don't know if I'm ready. Ready for what?" The thought of being "ready for what" finally just became an afterthought as I continued finishing up the desk. It was the third time, though.

There is no doubt that when God wants your attention, He will get it. I do have to admit that I still had lingering thoughts of the day before's message. "Are you ready?" Still I went on with my daily cleaning. I had noticed how time seemed to drag out forever this September month, unlike the entire rest of the year, which seemed like it had flown by. I spent this time waiting for Christopher's two big days. On September 12th, he would be heading off to the Marines, two days after turning 18 years old. On top of that, the kids would be returning to school, and there would be 101 things to do. What would make this month drag? I didn't know and didn't have time to figure it out. I was too busy getting ready for winter, so I thought.

The following morning was another sunny day so I set out to do the chores I had put off from the day before. During the weekdays when I am home alone, I make it my habit to sit down in front of the T.V. to watch the noon news and eat my lunch. This day wasn't any different other than one thing that I did. I decided I wasn't going to watch the news because I wanted to check on the football scores. I found the station I needed and pretty much in a tired daze sat on the living room floor in my work clothes and ate my lunch. I'd glance at the T.V. from time to time and listen for information that interested me. I did take notice of a commercial during one of the glances. I don't even remember what was being advertised, but I do remember one thing. In the commercial was a dog. The dog was wearing a blue T-shirt, and right at the end of the commercial, the dog looked directly at the camera and said, "Are you ready?" My mouth dropped open! Instantly, I reached for the remote control, turned off the T.V., and went directly into prayer.

Now I knew for sure that God was talking directly to me! No doubt in my mind! I prayed to God. "I don't know what it is that you want me to be ready for God, but here I am. I give myself over to you and I will humble myself to be prepared for whatever you have coming my way. Yes, God," I spoke with tears streaming down my face, "I am ready."

I sat on the floor looking across the room at the dining room wall. All it was to me was this big white space. It was like a blank canvas, and I had no idea what God was about to paint upon it. A hole in my life was going to be filled with what? Ready for what? Could it be my husband? Oh dear God, please don't let any harm come to my husband. Is it the house, the kids' issues at school? What Lord, what could it be? Then, in that moment, I decided again that I would trust in God. Trust God with whatever comes my way. God's ways are perfect and true and all for His glory, so why would I not trust Him? Doesn't our Bible say more

than once, "Do not fear"? Well, guess what? In order
to not fear whatever God puts in our path, we must
trust. In order to trust, we have to turn everything
in our lives over to God, better known as casting all
our cares, stepping out in faith, willing to take that
first step, and knowing that God is with you. Is this
easy? Of course not. You have to give it over to God
100%. You just can't say, "Well, maybe I'll trust you
a little and see what happens." You can't. God has to
be in control. It's like having Jesus take the wheel but
thinking you can keep your foot on the accelerator.
It doesn't work that way. It's more like, "Here, put on
this blindfold, and let me lead you wherever I want."
To trust, you have to let go of everything.

So, in that moment, that is what I decided. I chose
to trust God and bring forth what may. How would I
get through it? How would I make it to the other side?
Just go about my business and handle whatever comes
my way, the same as we're always taught. Handle
everything the way Jesus would. WWJD? If you don't
know, then the best way is to pick up your Bible and
get to reading. I still couldn't help but wonder what
it was that was going to be so important that God
would go through all that trouble to get my attention,

including blowing away the old wives' tale of things happening in threes. On that fourth time, I really knew He was trying to get my attention. I thought using a talking donkey was strange, but a dog? Thank you, Lord, that it was only on the T.V.

I did go about my business. I mean, once you make a direct commitment to God like that, all you can do is follow through and trust. How was I to know what God's timeline was? How was I to know that whatever I was supposed to be ready for was going to come a lot sooner than later? I wasn't to know. It wasn't but that following Saturday in the wee morning hours that the phone rang. A phone call that has changed my life and those around me forever.

I remember a couple of weeks before God told me to be ready for whatever that blank was to be filled with, thinking my life was in the best order it had been for awhile. I have to laugh at that. Living my life in a false truth. After all, my truth wasn't what I was thinking it was. This lesson had started on a Sunday. My husband, Red, has been delivering the sermons while our church is between pastors. This particular Sunday, he had given a message about tithing. During that message, he had mentioned that I was the one that handled the finances in our home. No big deal; it is just easier for me to take care of financial matters. I did think at some point during that message that I was pleased with how I had been able to stay on top of things this year. I had been able to take care of monthly bills *and* put aside money on a monthly basis for the big incoming bills, like house and auto insurance and property tax, things of that nature. I was even more pleased because I would be able to spend with ease whatever I wanted to at the Fryeburg Fair that we were planning to attend.

Well, wouldn't you know. Five days later, the wind was taken out of my sail. God knows how easy I can freak out, so he let me get a message on the answer machine so I would be able to get a grip before I approached this issue. It happened that on Friday morning, instead of doing my barn chores and coming directly into the house, I had decided to work on my stonewall that I was building as a splashguard against the barn. It truly amazes me how God puts those rocks together just like puzzle pieces. I find it comforting and peaceful to my soul to do this kind of work. The enjoyment was short-lived once I decided to see if anyone had called when I was outside. Sure enough, the message light was flashing. To my surprise it wasn't my husband or my neighbor. It was the bank. Did I hear that right? Did she say "overdraft"? What? I rewound the message and listened again. Overdraft! How could this be? I rushed out to my desk and found last month's checking statement, then went off to the bedroom to find my purse. With checkbook and checking statement in hand, I sat at the kitchen table and rechecked what I already knew matched up. Who cares if I never really balance the checkbook? I mean, who does, anyway? Everything checks off; how could this be happening? I decided to check and recheck my register and bank statement. Even then, my numbers and the bank's were in total agreement. I was shaking. My overdraft was more than $1,000! Everything matched; this just didn't make since. Could I be a victim of identity theft?

At that point, I decided to call my banker. Just two days before, I had to go out of town and use the bank I had always used before we moved to Bowerbank. God at work again, because the banker knew me and called me right away. If it was anyone else, I am sure that I would've just received all those notices in the mail. At her advisement, off to the local bank I went.

After spending over two hours with this kind and patient manager, we were still unable to pinpoint an exact mistake on my part. We did, however, come to a conclusion that I was writing down a wrong total in my register on the times I was getting cashbacks. I was forgetting to subtract that amount off of the total deposit. After making this mistake about three times, it was only discovered because of a large withdrawal with the check I had made out to the roofing company. That, along with other checks that I had written, caused the overdraft. Good thing this was found out so that I wouldn't continue to make the same mistake and not so good because I had to cover the overdraft. Thank you, God, that I was able to cover my mistake. Frustrated because it took all the money for the big bills I had set aside and would have to re-save. Wow! Did I ever feel foolish and humbled. I also had to pay for the log truck load of wood that same week. I thought that wasn't going to come until maybe the third week of October, but we all know that when it rains, it pours.

All this was part of God's plan, though. I didn't know it at the time, but God needed to do certain things in my life to put me where He wanted me to be. It wasn't going to be attending the Fryeburg Fair. That is why, after the money issue and feeling like a heel, I decided to talk to the kids about going to the Fryeburg Fair. I just told them straight up what I had done and that because of my errors it was going to mean having to tighten up on the budget. I didn't think our budget could handle the trip to the fair. I was surprised and relieved on how well they took it. We talked about things, and then we took a vote. We voted not to go to the fair. What a letdown. Throughout the entire summer, Red and I decided not to go to all the little fairs to just save that money so we could have one big fun outing. Mostly, this was my thought, and Red had agreed. Now the reality was this money issue.

That evening when Red called I told him that I had spoken to the children and that we had all voted that it was okay not being able to make it to our favorite fair until next year.

He said, "What about me and my vote? Don't I get a vote? How about all the fairs we didn't go to? I never get to do what I want, the one day I want, and now you say we can't go. Don't worry about the money; we'll still go."

I wasn't happy to hear any of this. I told him that I know me, and there was no way I would be able to go to the fair and enjoy myself knowing I wouldn't be able to just spend money on whatever I wanted and would have to worry about being thrifty the entire time I was there. I wanted to buy Christmas gifts as well, and now that would be totally out of the question with my ways of thinking. So no, I didn't want to go. We decided we would talk about it over the weekend. God had a plan, though, and the fair wasn't part of it.

I do remember thinking about the checkbook issue the day it happened. I had an extremely clear thought. A thought that was so clear it could've only been from God. That thought "Lean on me, Amber; lean on me." Wasn't I though? Was I really finding my security in our money? Really, wow, I didn't think or feel that I was. Leaning means you have to trust. After all, if you lean on someone and they move, you could fall. If I fall, I could get hurt, and who wants to hurt? It's you though, Lord, and I am willing to take that risk, to trust you and to lean on you. I've learned and read too many times in the Bible that God will never leave us; He will be there always, so I chose in that moment to say, "Yes Lord, I will lean on you."

Again, God was working directly in my life. He had prepared my heart and mind for the fact that I wasn't going to be at my favorite fair this year, and I even mentioned this to Red, that perhaps God just didn't want us going this year. Even if Red had already put in for a day off, it wouldn't have mattered if he were to show up at work, anyway. Skipping the fair wasn't even difficult. The lesson God was trying to get across was to lean on Him. The only problem was that I didn't know exactly for what reason. I thought it was for trusting in Him for all things and to lean on Him, not the checkbook, for our support. I was off with more than my math at this point.

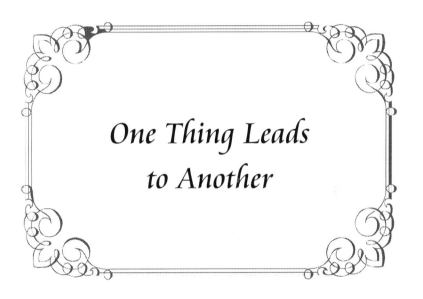

One Thing Leads
to Another

L et me take advantage of this moment to tell you about the property we found in Maine.

One afternoon, I was checking out the local advertisement flyer that came in the mail bi-weekly. I'd been wanting a Bernese mountain dog for about six years, so I was checking the paper for them. I happened upon an advertisement for 10 acres of land in Maine for around $15,000. Well, in this day and age, that is a steal. Red and I had been discussing getting a place up north as a vacation retreat, but mostly we had been considering buying something in New Hampshire. We decided to check this place out, along with a few other properties Red discovered on the Internet. He had decided to make a long day trip out of it.

We met up with a man in Bangor who gave us directions and pictures of the property. We then had to drive another hour and a half northeast. This was the last piece of property we had on our list to visit. The drive home just became longer, but as it turned out, it was worth the trip.

The road to the property was a dirt road, which gave a wonderful feeling of being out in the country like I was when I was growing up. We arrived at the

10 acres of property for sale but were disappointed to discover that a majority of the land was hillside. It just wasn't what we were looking for.

On the way out, we wanted to see where the rest of the road went and decided to take a left turn and explore. Turned out it became a dead end, and someone had their home built there. You could see by the fields and line of maple trees that at one time, it was someone's farmland. We quickly turned around and headed out.

As we drove out toward the main road, there was an oncoming truck. We decided to flag down the truck. Red spoke to the man for almost half an hour. We learned that this man owned the house at the end of the road and the ranch home we had passed on our way to the 10 acres, which was his mom's home. During the conversation, he had asked if we were up looking at another property that was vacant but not yet on the market. He also told us he was the one that had sold the man from Bangor the 10-acre property. Having been told about the second vacant property after the conversation, we decided that while we were there, we might as well go check it out. We were told the property was about 150 acres and had a newer house and an old camp with out buildings. It was worth looking anyway.

We drove into this long driveway, which over the years had grown grass over most of it. The drive turned into a loop as you approached the house. There was also around the loop the old camp and two out buildings. In the distance, it appeared that at one time, there was also a chicken coop. The grass was tall and overgrown, but we got out to look around just the same.

Red and I walked around some, then checked out the condition of the outside of the house. The house itself was covered in white vinyl siding. Not too pretty. There were grasshoppers jumping every which way, and deer flies swarmed around our heads like mad, but that didn't dissuade our curiosity. I had Red put me on his shoulders so I could see through the backdoor window. We would've used the steps, but Red already tried, and they cracked under his weight.

Right away, and I mean right away, I said, "Red, this is our place!" All I could see of the inside were cedar-paneled walls. Loved it! I didn't know why, but I just had this overwhelming feeling of this house being ours. We peeked in a few more windows, and still the excitement grew. We could see the kitchen, dining room, and living room area; we were enamored by its beautifully built granite chimney. Loved it! A loft! Loved it! Wow, could we really have this place? Let the footwork begin!

It was July of 2004 when all this started taking place. Over a year later, we were still trying to find information to get in touch with the landowner. We looked on the Internet to find the phone number to the town hall in Carroll, Maine. I spoke with a woman who informed me that she was the town's tax collector and that the property tax hadn't been paid for the last four years. She couldn't seem to find the owners, either. She ended up giving us the name of a relative that would possibly be able to give us some information. We sent out a certified letter, which was returned to us. At that point, we just decided to wait. We thought maybe in December, when tax bills started going out, that something would happen. It got to be January when I mentioned to Red that by now, the tax bills should have gone out. I got the go-ahead to make my phone call to up north.

It turned out to be quite a phone call. I was informed by the tax collector that just the week before, she had received all the back taxes on the property that we were interested in. She was also informed by the owner, from Texas, that if anyone was interested in the property to let him know. Otherwise, the property was going on the market come April. What timing! God at work. I took down the phone number of the landowner and gave it to Red so that he could make the call. The tax collector said she would also call and let the landowner know our names and give him our phone number. Hurray! The wheels were in motion.

One Sunday afternoon, we received our long-awaited phone call from the landowner. Red offered him a price for the property, and he accepted. Just like that! We landed 156 acres with a camp for $60,000. What a deal! The landowner told Red he was just in charge of the estate and had never stepped foot on the property and just wanted to get rid of it. Lucky us!

It all turned into another waiting game. It took almost four months just to get a fax of the deed. We later found out it was because the landowner's secretary got cancer. He needed to find a temporary fill-in, and that slowed business down in his office. He was a lawyer.

Red started his part of the paper shuffle on our end. He found lawyers in Connecticut and Maine in order to get this business completed. Just getting our loan approved and signing a lot of paperwork would be our final steps in this long, drawn-out process.

The entire experience had been a trial. All the waiting made me think it was all in God's timing. I've never heard of such circumstances happening to others. I can't help but believe that God had His plan working here. We didn't get disappointed or overly excited; we just let it be what it was. God used my desire for wanting a dog to place us in our vacation getaway.

We didn't plan on moving up there, but I was excited and was looking forward to happy memories at our new place.

Maine Adventure

A fter careful consideration we decided to move up to Carroll, Maine! July 30, 2007! Now, here I sit four plus years later with a heavy heart. Funny how time has a way of filling in the blanks of your life. I remember being so glad to put the state of Connecticut behind me. With all that went on with Red...whew...what a tangled web. He made it through his cancer operation, a divorce, reuniting with his firstborn son, his breaking away from the shipyard he had worked at most of his life, his two back operations, and one thing after another with the children. It just seemed never ending. We decided together that it would be best to move north. What a ride it would become.

When we had first decided to even think about moving, Red and I had talks, of course, about whether this would be the best decision, whether or not it was better to raise the children in city limits as opposed to all the outdoors Maine had to offer. Then, we also had our prayers. It came down to this: if God wanted it to be, then the doors would open. After all, the way the property in Maine came into our lives was strange to begin with, the overwhelming feeling I experienced while looking into the windows was something I couldn't ignore, and the way the phone calls had gone with the taxes all just added up as a "move ahead" moment. It was decided; here we come, Maine. More like, "Watch out, Maine; here come the Bartlett Boys!" Oh my.

Making the decision to move seemed like the easy part knowing what was in front of me. What was in front of me was a huge wall of stuff. I've never in my life known anyone who owned so much stuff as Red. We had had talks in the past about hoarding, but Red wasn't on the same page as me about the subject, yet. Lucky for me one of his back operations took place around this time.

We knew that when the children finished up with the school year that we would head to Maine. I am one that doesn't like to wait last minute to prepare, so I decided to start packing for the move in mid-February. I just went through the house and packed things that we didn't have to use on an everyday basis. It also gave me the opportunity to unload what I thought to be all the unnecessary things in our lives. Winter passed, which opened up the doors to start moving things on the outside of the house. Now, when I say open doors, I literally mean open doors. Opening up the doors to our storage bin, the door on the house garage, the two garage doors on the workshed, and last but certainly not least was an 18-wheeler storage container that his mom had stuff in from her family! For someone that doesn't like clutter like myself, this was a nightmare, but knowing I could disperse it out into the world was a dream come true.

Along with our oldest son, Christopher, I decided to tackle the 18-wheeler storage unit first. Yuck! Things had been in there for years untouched. It was interesting in one aspect to see things from the past, and I believe Chris enjoyed the feeling of being on a treasure hunt. I'd have to remind him at times to just stay in one area at a time. We dug ourselves into all that was there and were relieved when we were able to make a path to walk in. We discovered along the way that the ceiling had a few leaks, and you know what that means! Mold. Both of us were none too pleased with that. Underneath the leaks were lots and lots of books, moldy books. Many things had to go in the dumpster, and we both ended up getting sick over it. We plugged away, though, and got the job done. God tells us to store up on our treasures in Heaven, where they can't become destroyed, and not on material things, lest our hearts be there also. These material things we store can sometimes be pointless. I knew right in that moment the things Chris and I had to dispose of had become nothing but a waste of time and energy. Then for us to get sick on top of it was our reward. I kept myself focused on the bright side, which was just not having it any longer. God has a way of cleaning up our lives, doesn't He?

The two-door garage shed that Red had built was supposed to be a work area for him. However, like every other space, it was filled with stuff. I went through it, but mostly it was his to shuffle through. That was pretty much it as far as the house garage went, also.

That left the storage unit up at the front of the property to go through. The local thrift shop must've loved me then. I made at least five trips with the minivan crammed full and made lots of people happy with those items. Then, there were many items that were set out at the side of the road with a nice bright neon orange sign announcing "Everything here you see is FREE!" It was like Christmas for all who wanted to share in it. I love to give people things, so this was a great way to get some satisfaction out of all my hard work.

When I first began this task, I would pray to God and ask Him how in the world we were going to get rid of all this stuff we don't need? It was crazy! One item that I had man-handled out to the side of the pickup truck bed, which was also up for grabs, was an extremely heavy, handmade, wooden workbench.

I said to Red, "Who in the world would want this?"

"Someone will," he reassured me.

"Yeah right," was my thought on that. There we were, all this stuff in the yard with our "FREE" sign. We decided to leave the house and go grocery shopping. If someone stopped by for something, it would be pretty much self-explanatory. Besides, human nature would make it easier for someone to help themselves if no one was looking. That would be fine with me, but remember what God says; He is with us always and sees everything we do.

It was no longer than two hours when we returned home from our grocery shopping. I couldn't help but glance over at everything in the yard to see if anyone took interest in our unwanted belongings. To my dismay, there still appeared to be quite a lot there. However, when we got out of the car, we did notice that one item was gone. It was the wooden workbench! At that moment, I knew God was telling me not to worry, that He would handle everything. I still get a chuckle out of this.

Another larger item that we wanted to get rid of was my first motorcycle that Red had bought me for a birthday present. It was a 250 Honda Rebel. Red took it a little more seriously than I did when I spoke about my desire to have my own street bike, because then the reality was having to ride it. This hadn't been a huge problem for me to overcome, being I was raised riding dirt bikes. However, I'd have to go to class to obtain my motorcycle license, and that was where my confidence had faltered. Red decided after all those years that he would get his motorcycle license, too. That had made the entire ordeal much more fun. We both passed the class, and I even received a higher grade than him. Believe me, though, that had by no means made me a better driver.

The Honda wasn't something that we were going to put a "FREE" sign on, so once again, I was wondering if we were going to get rid of that, as well. As God would have it, He would remind me again that He was in control of all things and I need not be overly concerned with any matter. I had once before had the motorcycle out for sale with no interest from anyone. In the garage it went with everything else. This second time was God's timing, and He had the bike sold on the third day! The man who bought it said he had seen it before winter and had an interest, but now with the gas prices rising, he wanted something just to get back and forth to work with. I found it comical that the bike looked so tiny under his six-foot plus height. Guess the price was good enough that he didn't mind. One more item down, thank you Lord.

Through the days, God worked His wonders, and eventually, items just kept leaving the property. Our neighbor must've thought he struck it big when we asked if he wanted Red's old pickup truck from his dad, a pile of scrap copper, firewood we weren't going to use, a huge pile of red bricks, a large amount of cinder blocks, a refrigerator, a futon frame, and various other items from the house. Like I said, Red had a lot of things.

Another young man couldn't believe it when he stopped to ask if the pickup bed was really for free or if we were just using it to hold up our "FREE" sign. That was funny. He was happy to hear that it was free to take because he had a friend in need of it. I asked him if he minded taking the metal cabinet that was in the back of it. Off he went with both. Hurray! That meant it was all gone.

God teaches us that we should give and help the poor and needy but to do it with a joyful heart. I have to say, I received joy just knowing that all the items were gone. Yes, I was trusting God that He would see to it that it would be gone, but along with enjoying helping people out, I have to admit there were selfish intentions. We need to remember not to have those selfish intentions when we do for others, because that is only pleasing to ourselves and not God.

Still, to this day, we have things packed in boxes from our move from Connecticut to Maine. The only difference is that now, Red is on the same page with me about getting rid of some more stuff. That's great, though. It has only been four years, but like they say: better late than never.

We settled into our new home in Maine, which was quite different from our home in Connecticut. Our new home came without electrical power, which meant we had to use a generator. The first year, we used a generator that wasn't meant for long-term use, so I could do a great commercial for that company. Our heat came from a used wood stove that Red had picked up in Connecticut. It was also used to dry our clothes, which I hung in the basement. Our second winter, Red built another wood stove, which kicked out too much heat! We would walk around in shorts and open the windows with that one. Red built it so it would heat our water, and I still cooked on the stovetop even though we had purchased a gas stove. I actually enjoyed my one-pot meals that I cooked on that stove. Even though things were a bit different from our previous living conditions, I was always thankful for what God had provided for us. Counting my blessings is just one thing I was taught from church.

Our first spring is when I decided to get my first goat, Betsy. After all, we had a plan to become "self-sufficient," the reason why we didn't care so much about the no electrical power issue. Betsy was pregnant when I bought her, and she kidded out one pure white male. I named him Poppy. I thought I was well on my way to having our own milk and meat. I bought Daisy, a purebred boar doe, to breed with Poppy, which is where the meat would come from. Over the course of two and a half years, I found myself becoming a shepherd to a herd of ten goats. That is how I'd spend much of my time. It just got sappy. Really.

When it was all said and done, I gave them all away, except Charley. Oh, what a guilt trip that sent me on. I called a man, and he came over and looked at all my goats. He agreed to take them off my hands, so less than a week passed, and away they all went. All five! Boy, did I cry. Dolly and her kid Jessey went to a friend, and Frosty and Dusty went to another woman in town. Charley stayed with me.

I really did try to give Charley away. I had called a man in town that had a 4H going on to see if he could stay there. Back and forth Charley went until I just decided to keep him home. My second attempt on giving him away resulted in me going to pick him up two days later and bringing him home yet again. Now here I am 18 months later, and I still have Charley. Not only that, but my friend gave me back Jessey so Charley would have a friend, and then Dolly because she wasn't producing enough milk to keep on the milking farm. Since then, however, I've had to put Dolly down because she became lame. That's farm talk for making the choice to send her to the grave.

Choices like that are never pleasant, but in a situation such as that, I thought it was the wisest route.

If I had listened to God in the first place, I would never have had to be in the face of that horrible decision to begin with, which makes me wonder what other things in my life I wouldn't have had to go through if I had only listened to God's leading, even the times when the solution was made so clear to me.

I remember clearly the time when God told me to get rid of my goats. I had been out taking my herd for a walk and browsing time. As I headed back in the direction of the house, I had begun to talk with God. I was talking with Him about Moses and the Israelites, which led into talking about sacrifice and how, when we did sacrifice, we were to give up our best. I ended up busting out in tears because I was so aware in that moment that if I were to give up my best, it would be Charley and Dolly. I asked, "Is that what you want me to do God? Give up my best?" I knew God was asking me to give up my goats. Cry! Boy did I cry! This was my life, and these were my kids; why God are you asking me to do this?

That's how I ended up still having goats. It all boiled down to me not being obedient to God.

I knew with all my heart that I had let the goats become a roadblock to what God wanted to work in my life, and as long as I held onto them, I couldn't move forward. I asked my husband to call the butcher shop, only for me to call and cancel the appointment. I should've just listened to God in the first place, and Charley would've been in the trailer along with everyone else, and this wouldn't have come to such heartache. I have him up for sale, and I'm hoping the phone will ring soon.

Our second move here to Bowerbank was what created all this goat talk. I was just plain tired of living out in the woods and wanted to live, not just survive all the time. I wanted a home with real electricity, and I wanted the children to have fun in the summer, not use that time to have to prepare for winter.

We wanted to be more in a central location in the state of Maine. This would allow for Red to travel back and forth to work daily in order to be home more to help with the care of the children. Having three teenage boys is no easy task.

At first, Chris didn't want to move, and David wanted to stay near his friends. Priscilla said she'd miss her friends, and I don't recall Bradley's reaction. I wanted a bigger home, and like I said, real electricity. So, here we are. We are on the north side of Sebec Lake, a place Red came to visit as a child. We have a three bedroom, two bath log home. We are on the opposite side of the road from the lake, so we hear our taxes are lower. We also live on a dead end road just like back in our previous home. The children have enjoyed riding their bikes and go swimming down at the boat landing one and a half miles away.

Our first summer here was the first summer we've actually all enjoyed. Chris took a job at Ames Construction, David worked part-time on a local farm doing mostly haying, and Bradley became my main helper. He also picked up a job mowing our part-time neighbor's yard and did pretty well picking up bottles along the roadside. Priscilla became a better swimmer, and we both enjoyed our fishing poles and boat outings. I even got a gingerbread suntan for the first time in years!

Still, our only big chore is firewood. We've completed one log truck load of firewood and still have yet another to complete. Life was just moving along.

Upon moving to Bowerbank, one of our biggest concerns was to find a church. We had tried attending one church, and that didn't work for us, so we had decided to move on. After attending the next church for a couple of months, the pastor decided to leave for financial reasons. Now of all things, Red is filling in. Yeah, really! The Bible teaches that God's ways are not our ways, and of this you can be sure.

It's quite interesting how we found this new church. I had been wanting some lamps for the living room. I knew that Red had good taste when it came to picking out things like that for the home, so I felt comfortable asking him if he would keep that in mind when he was out and about. During this time, we had also discussed finding a different church to attend.

The same week, Red had read an article in the newspaper about a new church that had opened. In his travels to and from work listening to the radio, he had heard an advertisement for log home furnishings. So off he went to the store, and wouldn't you know the wife of the pastor at the new church that had opened worked at the store. Serious! She ended up inviting us to visit their church. Red came home and told me this, and it was decided that we would give it a try. The church is a 40-minute drive from our home and is called New Beginnings Bible Church. How about that name, too? Wow! We felt comfortable with the church and decided to attend on a regular basis.

At this point, the church is still between pastors, so Red has ended up volunteering to give the messages. Now God is using Red to give the Sunday message! Amazing to say the least. Interesting to see God at work. This by no means, however, means that life is perfect. God is working here, but that is only because He is preparing us. For what? For the things unseen, the things we give no thought to because we are just living. Living and thinking we're in control, and all the while it is God who is moving us. We believed we were at the church we should be in and found our furnishings. The lamp/church incident was just to strange to ignore.

Right Side Up Just
Went Upside Down

T hat's one thing about life: it's always moving forward. Regardless. Maintain normalcy. I had actually been giving thought to changing my normal. But normal molds itself into our lives, and before we know it, we stop and wonder what happened to "those days." I don't want them back; I continue to have the desire to grow and keep moving forward. That means I haven't given up, and that means I am living. I just want to be what God wants me to be and go where He wants me to go. With that desire comes change. With change, we learn, sometimes quickly, that we aren't in control. Not totally. This is God's world, and His will will be done. Growing pains you may get, but joy you will receive. As long as we walk in His ways.

I know I've been stubborn in the last few years. I believe God wanted me more advanced in my walk for reasons that have been revealed to me as of late. I could've listened; it was like I wasn't hearing. Just a brat doing things my way, not willing to change when called to. What's that saying? "If you want to make God laugh, tell Him your plans."

Well, I don't think God was laughing at my plans. I think He probably got quite frustrated with me at times. He did get my attention at one point and I've grown since then, but even I'm aware I'm not where I want to be with my growth.

So life kept moving. Even though I was having better times, I still lived with my old frustrations. You know there are things that you just want to get past already, but because others are creating them, they just never seem to go away. You try every avenue to get people past things, but they just keep holding on to their same old behaviors.

David is a living example of this. He has a problem helping himself to things that aren't his. Then, on top of that come the lies. On top of that, he gets caught and still lies. On top of that, he gets caught and lies some more. This has been this way *forever*! Finally, he had a great opportunity to earn money and be trusted to ride his bike to work. What did he do? Rode his bike to the local mom and pop store and shoplifted. On another occasion, he came home with a clock radio that he said he stole from a camper down the street, and the man that owned the camper said it wasn't his clock radio. So where did it come from? He still hasn't told us to this day.

Christopher had his full-time job, too. Great! Even so, every time he'd come home, he'd give me tons of disrespect and a negative attitude. I know it was because he thought he didn't need me anymore. Sick of rules and almost 18, he just wanted to be on his own.

Bradley and Priscilla's biggest problem was bickering, which I had hoped would've lessened after not having the two oldest around. Wishful thinking. Overall though, they were great and had lots of fun in our new neighborhood.

I figured Chris would soon be off to the Marines, and the other three would be back in school. I figured David would finally start caring enough about his future and pass his classes. I thought Bradley would dive head-first into his new enthusiasm of being a freshman. Priscilla being older, I thought she'd learn to stop talking so much.

Yeah right! Chris quit the Marines one week before he was scheduled to depart. David is flunking all but two classes. Bradley is also flunking classes, and Priscilla seems to be still thinking she can talk about family stuff and it's okay. Some of it is, but she talks to the point of invading other people's privacy. With David, it just figures. My hands are thrown up in the air sometimes. It seems he just doesn't care. Personally, I believe he has just been passed through the school system for one reason or another. Even now, they are going to put him in what they call the alternative classes. That is a class with fewer students so the teacher can work one-on-one with each of them. This will allow David to get things handed to him and passed through school once again. His back is up against the wall, and he is getting caught in his own web. Wait until the real world. This is only a speck of the frustrations growing in my life. That is why we are to remain close to God with prayer and stay in His word, so that we remain strong in our storms. We only can be in control of ourselves.

The way we believe life will move is not always going to be our reality. We have our hopes and dreams and wishes for ourselves and children, but for one reason or another, they get changed for you. Like Christopher with the Marines. I've always planted seeds along the years that the military would be a good route for these boys. I believed in my heart that it would give them direction in their lives. Chris came to a point where he finally got it together in school and set goals for himself. He wanted to work with heavy equipment through the Marines, I believe as a mechanic. That was going to happen for him. Chris also got his CDL through school. Chris seemed to be headed in what I thought was a good direction. Then *bam!* While he started to pack up his room to what I thought was going in storage, Chris informed me he wasn't going into the Marines. What? When did this happen? He had quit the day before! WHAT?

Yes, I freaked. I told Chris loudly exactly what I thought. Furthermore, when I questioned Christopher about why he had quit, he just smirked and laughed. This only frustrated me even more. He didn't have an answer for me. I continued to question him. Did he think his job was so great he didn't need to further his education? Was it a girl? He crunched his face disgusted that I would even consider a girl having a hold of him which reassured me that wasn't the case. Well, what was it, then? More smirks. I walked away. I went upstairs and called the recruiter.

The recruiter explained to me how Christopher came in to quit and how they spent five hours trying to change his mind. Finally, after a display of rude and disrespectful behavior the "big guy" told him to get out of his office, that they didn't need his kind. That was it, discharged. Seemed like all my hopes for Chris were just flushed away. All I wanted for him was a solid start to his future. I prayed the Marines would spot his anger issues and work them out of him somehow. I just wanted him to work hard at something for himself and rid that anger out so he could enjoy his life. Gone, all of it, just gone. How would he get past that anger now? All I could think of was my brother and how all he ever was was miserable. King of grump. I didn't want that for Chris. Now, maybe years would pass before it was worked out. What did this teach me? I was mad! I was disgusted! I wanted to wring his neck for being what I thought was the stupidest move of his life he'd make. To me, he was throwing away his future. I kept my distance from Chris the remainder of the day.

That distance continued on into Sunday when we arrived at church. I was still fuming. I even made a point in sitting a row away from him because I just didn't want to sit next to him. Chris always made a point of sitting next to me each Sunday.

The church had a going away card for Chris. That's when he stood and announced to everyone he wasn't leaving for the Marines. People were shocked,

I just sat there all stiff and fuming. Chris never got the card.

However, in that very moment God said, "See, Amber, this is free will. You are trying to show Chris the best path to give him a great life, and there's nothing you can do to change his mind. *Nothing!* That's what it's like for me, child of mine, when I try to make you see my way is the best way and you choose your way. There is *nothing* I can do to change that choice because *I, Me, God,* created free will and you who exercise it."

Wow! Has my own free will caused God to feel these things: frustration, disappointment, hurt, sorrow, even tears maybe, angry maybe. Let it go. Let Christopher go. Let him live his life and be who he chooses to be. I could only hope for the best.

That was Sunday, September 4th, 2011. On Saturday, September 10th, 2011, Chris had his 18th birthday. He wanted to move out, and I wanted him out. I thought, go ahead, big shot! Now go see what the world has to offer. Low-paying job and having to work extra hours to bring home a halfway decent paycheck. Only day off you have is Sunday. Bought a piece of junk truck from the boss, which I'm sure he was glad to be rid of. Now what? Like I told you last weekend, don't bring your drama to my doorstep. Oh, and admitting out loud how now I'd be worried about him! For what? He told me I didn't have to worry. REALLY?

Go on and go. Take your know-it-all ways and your negative attitude and go be angry somewhere else. I have three more to grow and guide; I just don't need this. Furthermore, you don't want to be here, and you'd be too stubborn to admit it if you wanted to stay. Such a typical parent/teenager episode.

A week later while I was vacuuming the living room carpet, I wondered what that was all for, anyway. I missed Chris during the summer, and I missed him when he left. I only got over it by reminding myself what a negative attitude he gave me. Filling in the hole of hurt with anger. Chris and I were alike in that way. I worried that I had taught him that, but no, I wouldn't take full responsibility over that. There was a lot in his life even before I showed up.

Within that timeline of a week, a lot was learned, from walking completely in the flesh to getting the extreme free will lesson from God. I knew Chris had found a place to stay with a guy at work and came to the conclusion that it's his life. It was just going to be different, and I would just have to go with it. Whatever may come.

For those of you who aren't familiar with the phrase "walking in the flesh," let me try to clear that up. In simple terms, it means not living your life in a Christ-like manner, not living and making decisions using God's rules and ways. Basically, just shooting off at the mouth and letting your feelings lead you where they may.

That past Friday evening, September 9th, Red had a heated discussion with Chris. It didn't start out a pretty picture. Chris was giving Red snotty comments, and Red wasn't too pleased with this behavior. Not good.

I didn't want things to continue this way for either of them, not a memory of fighting and name calling his last night at home. I interrupted after Red had said a few things. Earlier, when we were alone, Red had asked me not to say anything while he had his conversation with Chris, nor did he inform me of what he was to talk about. I was not sorry for interrupting and talking for over 15 minutes straight. I'm still not! For both of their sakes.

Red never cut me off or asked me to be quiet, and Chris's tears of frustration stopped flowing. I spoke only truth to Chris as I saw it. I only asked him to do his best, and then Red talked. In the end, they hugged each other and told each other they loved one another. That was such a good thing to be a witness of. I wanted that for them when it could've so easily went the other way. I thank God for that moment.

I also thank God for another moment, which took place the next day, Christopher's birthday. His big day, turning 18, a day he thought would never get there, and a day I often screamed I wished had already come. So, what is a boy to think? "Freedom! Take your rules and shove 'em! Independence! I'll do it my way!" Is it any wonder? I couldn't even wait for 18; I ran away from home at 17. I heard from David that Chris was out the door at 12:01 a.m. I laughed. Whatever. It came as no surprise to me when he came upstairs that morning

We had a small celebration of his coming of age the evening before. Red gave him a card, and I gave Red the suggestion of getting Chris a safe so he could lock up all his important stuff. Of course, Red got him a nice one. The thing is heavy too.

I try to sleep in on Saturdays being it's our only day to do so. I couldn't that morning, and my back was getting stiff lying in bed trying to go back to sleep. I decided just to get out of bed. I wandered out to the kitchen to make a pot of coffee. Chris came up while it was brewing. I felt like he gave me that "Oh, you're up" look. I let it pass and asked if he wanted to have a cup of coffee together before he took off. He said no, he had to go meet up with someone, then went off to use the bathroom. I stopped him on his way downstairs, and he didn't seem to mind. I thought he was moving slow for someone who couldn't wait to be gone.

We talked. Mostly me, which is nothing new. I gave him the "Do it God's way" talk, "Be Smart" talk, and much to his discomfort, the "Sex" talk. I just didn't want him to go that road and make things even more difficult for himself. He assured me he'd be smart. Then, much to our surprise, we hugged. Chris actually picked me off the floor and gave me a bear hug. What was this? He headed down the stairs. I called out to him to make wise choices.

"I will." His last words to me before heading toward his freedom.

During our conversation, I had mentioned to him that he should slow down while driving his truck. When he pulled out of the driveway slower than the norm, I wondered if he was taking my advice or having apprehensions of being on his own. Chris reassured Red a couple weeks later when Red called to check on him that life was everything he expected it would be. Chris wouldn't admit it if it wasn't. That's why I put off calling him. I thought that if I did, he'd be too "busy" to except a dinner invitation. He might even toss out an "I don't know. Who's cooking?" I let it go and tried to give him his space.

Forever Changed

ctober 1st, 2011, God put His truth straight in my face again, and this time it would change my world forever. That is when I was woken up by my phone ringing at 12:35 a.m.

I came out in a daze to the kitchen to answer the phone. I was too slow; I missed it. Within seconds my cell phone started ringing. Who in the world could be calling my cell phone so late? Not many people have that number, let alone try calling right after not getting me on the house phone. Could it be my best friend, my sister, my son from out of state? Who? My thoughts buzzed quickly in my tired mind as I flipped open my cell phone. I didn't bother to look at the phone number on the front screen.

"Hello?"

"Is this Amber?"

"Yes?"

It was the sheriff.

"Yes!"

"I have been trying to call you. You need to come to the hospital. Chris has been in an accident. It's pretty bad. Do you understand?"

"Yes, which hospital?"

"Mayo Hospital in Dover-Foxcroft."

"Thank you."

I hung up, my mind and body going into emergency mode. I had to wake Red. (Can this guy ever catch a break with his sleep?) I didn't want to be a bearer of bad news. A phone call we never wanted and were somehow expecting. Numb, I gently brushed Red's arm.

"Red. Red, wake up. I have to tell you something."

"Yeah, yeah, what?"

"It's Chris. The sheriff called and said we have to go to Mayo Hospital right now."

"What happened?"

"Chris has been in an accident. He says it's bad. We have to hurry up."

We got dressed and headed out. It was about a 30-minute drive. Red drives cautiously anyway, but I wondered why of all times he was doing the speed limit. We stayed calm, and we spoke some, but I'd have to dig real deep to even remember what we said to one another. Finally, we got to the hospital. Just as we were parking, a helicopter approached its landing.

"Do you think that's for Chris, Red?"

"Probably so."

I took off running to the entrance of the ER. There's a couple and hospital staff. I see the sheriff. He shows me where Chris is. I hurry in and go up to his left side.

"Chris, your father is here."

I wanted Chris to know his father was there in his time of need. I knew he was aware of who was speaking to him. I turned to Red, who was standing with the sheriff in the doorway. Did he come over in that moment? I can't remember. Next thing I knew, the sheriff was saying something.

"The parents of the girlfriend are over in the other room."

I had no idea or even cared to know who they were at that moment. Chris was my only thought.

"The parents are over here."

"I don't know them." I think he repeated himself; I know I did. "I don't know them!"

Red left with the sheriff. I turned back to Chris. I reached out and touched his exposed foot. His feet were cold! Everyone, everywhere, doing so much. At some point, they told me they sedated him. Tubes, scratches, bruises, blood everywhere. I stepped back so as not to interfere with what work needed to be done. Red came back at some point. We were in and out of the room.

Talk was happening about flying Chris to Eastern Maine Medical in Bangor. We needed to get the other three children. We needed to get gas. I didn't want to be away from Chris. I tried to stay calm, tried to stay rational. We left and went to the nearby gas station. We went back to the hospital. Chris was still there. I guess they wanted to make sure Chris was stable before taking a flight. We really didn't know. Finally, they gave it a go. We were to meet up with Chris in Bangor.

We went home to get the children. We spoke on the ride home. I don't know what about. We got home and gathered up the children. They said they had been awake when we had left the first time. I wish they had said something; we could already be on our way to Bangor. Didn't change anything. We got in the car and began our journey to Bangor. The trip would take at least an hour. At that point, Red told the children what was happening.

Chris has been in a car accident. He had been coming home from Bangor with his girlfriend, and he fell asleep at the wheel. They hit a pine tree head on. He was driving her car. The discussion continued…

"Whose car?"

"What is her name?"

"What was he doing in Bangor?"

"Was he speeding?"

"Is Chris okay?"

"Is his girlfriend okay?"

"Who?"

"What?"

"What?"

"What?"

Calm answers, then a lot of quiet. Had to stay calm, stay calm. This was in God's hands. Had to stay calm, breathe. It was in God's hands.

All that information that the children were given had come from the girlfriend's stepfather. He had approached Red and me outside the emergency room entrance while we were waiting for them to decide on Chris's Life Flight. I hadn't gone to introduce myself with Red and the sheriff earlier, and it was in that moment I told the stepfather about how frustrated I felt. I didn't hold back, and I know I disappointed God. I just let it fly right out of my mouth.

"I don't know you guys. I'm also irritated with this girlfriend because it was less than a week ago that I even knew she existed, and existed as Chris's girlfriend at that! Furthermore, I was told by David she was bragging at school how it was because of her that Chris didn't join the Marines!" So yeah, my blood was boiling, and I didn't want anything to do with them.

He had some kind words to say, but I didn't relent. At his departing he tried to hug me, but I didn't return the hug. "Don't touch me!" is what I wanted to scream. My body went stiff, and my heart was hardened. I wanted to tell him to just go away, that he was not part of my world.

Finally, we got to Eastern Maine Medical in Bangor. A long drive that passed in a blur. A confused walk to the entrance of the ER directed by detour signs. A short wait in the outer waiting room. We were given a private waiting room and offered some drinks. Wait, wait, wait.

I had to go to the bathroom. If there is one thing in life I've learned, it is to relieve the bladder when you have a chance. I went to find the bathroom that we were told was just down the hallway. Upon my return to the waiting room, I met a nurse apparently on his way to see us. He introduced himself to me and said a few things about Chris that I don't really remember.

Suddenly, there was Chris, on his way to an MRI. The nurse let me go over to see him. I did it quickly; every minute was important.

Together with the nurse, I went into the private waiting area. I sat, and then the nurse explained what was going on to the family. There would be a MRI to show any injuries Chris may have. We waited. At some point, a doctor came in and spoke with us, then off to speak with a neurologist. Wait, wait, wait, wait, and wait.

Results came. How can you prepare? I had already given this over to God, knowing it would all play out His way. Being a mom, I still had to make sure everyone else was okay. Red was quiet. David, Bradley, and Priscilla mostly were quiet. At times even then, they bickered about who was sitting where and whose drink was whose. My goodness, I was wishing they would give it a break already!

At last, the door opened. Now we'd know the extent of Chris's injuries. The doctor spoke, and we listened intently. Chris had two broken collar bones, a number of broken ribs in the upper chest, a damaged spleen, two damaged vertebrae in his lumbar region, and worst of all, a torn bronchial tube on the right lung, a collapsed left lung, and a bleeding brain. They told us the whats and whys, the ifs, the whats and whens. We did our best to understand with our confused, tired minds. All I wanted was to be near Chris. Could we see him, and when? Wait. Breathe. Stay calm. Wait. This was in God's hands.

They gave us the go ahead to see Chris. Red and I went first. The children came in after; Red had gone to get them. Doctors were everywhere. There was that usual yucky hospital smell. Suddenly, David said he felt like he was going to pass out.

"I don't feel good. I think I'm going to pass out."

I told him to sit down on the floor. David stumbled backward.

"Red, grab him!"

David was rushed out of the room. People rushed over to get him a chair. Eventually, he returned to the waiting room. Bradley and Priscilla followed not too long after. Red went with them, and I stayed with Chris. A doctor came in to stitch up Chris's right elbow.

Red and I had noticed this gash at Mayo Hospital. How could that have happened? I had to leave the room while his elbow was being stitched. I went to the bathroom. I sat down outside in a chair waiting with a cup of coffee. Someone along the line had offered to get me a cup. I knew it was to be a long day ahead, so I did not refuse. At one point, Red came in; he took my spot in the chair, and I returned to the waiting room so that the children wouldn't have to be alone. We waited and we wondered.

Tests had been completed, and decisions had been made. Chris was going to be moved into ICU while trying to figure out why the brain was bleeding and not operate on his injuries until it could be decided if he was stable enough or if it was even worth the while.

The family headed to the ICU waiting area. We settled in. We waited. By then, it was headed into Saturday afternoon. The children were growing restless. They even said they were bored. I told them I was sorry, but that was the least of my concerns at that time. I told them to watch the T.V. or play on the computer that was provided in the waiting rooms. Something!

Chris was settled into ICU, and we finally got to go see him. We went in; tubes and beeping machines were our welcome mat. Red got on his knees and prayed. Bradley and Priscilla were there, and David stayed near the entrance. Back to the waiting room. Back and forth from Chris to the other children. At some point, people we knew started showing up from our church. We talked, hugged, and cried. It gave relief from the stress. I wanted to visit; I wanted to be with Chris.

More decisions. What to do with the children? God provides! Priscilla went with a family from church. She was going to go to a football game that they were headed to. They just happened to have an extra ticket to the football game, so they said she would then spend the night and attend church with them the next morning. This was a great relief because I wanted her to be able to have that distraction. Thank you, God.

David went with Chris's friend Cupcake to spend the night at his house. We gave David some money for dinner and sent him on his way. I was uncomfortable with these plans but knew it was necessary. I only hoped in the middle of all that was going on that we didn't get another phone call concerning David. I sent up a prayer on that one.

Bradley would have to stay with me for now. Later, when I had to go home to care for the animals, I would drop Bradley off at the home of a neighbor

Chris had been friendly with. They had two sons, and I thought Bradley was going to feel comforted with them being that they were friends with Chris.

I had to make the drive home so I could take care of my pets. I had a dog, two cats, and two goats. This would mean an hour's trip home, and then back again alone. I had noticed the weather outside was rainy and windy. My worst night driving weather.

I'd have to drive, and I did. With God's strength, I stayed strong in that moment. I had to get home, and no way was I going to not keep Bradley safe. I stopped at our neighbor's, thanking God she was already home from going out of town. I explained Chris's condition and asked if she'd take care of the animals until I knew when we'd be home. She agreed, thank God again.

Bradley and I got home and got clothes for him and David. I packed an overnight bag for Red and myself. We got the animals all fed and headed back out. I thanked God again that my dog didn't mess the floor. I arrived at the neighbor's and dropped off Bradley. Now I was alone. I had an hour's trip ahead of me. It was still raining and windy. I had no radio in my vehicle. I was alone with my own thoughts. I prayed to God to keep me safe. My phone rang. It was my best friend! God provides. She stayed on the phone with me most of my ride.

Back in the hospital parking lot, I grabbed up all our stuff and struggled under the weight of what I had packed. There was a line at the front door, and I thought they had to be kidding. Security guards were handing out passes to after-hour visitors. I saw Red headed toward the stairway. Must have been going to get something to eat.

"Red!" He stopped and turned. "Red!" He turned back around and headed up the stairs. My heart sank. I waited. Just breathe. It was only a policy for safety's sake.

My turn! They took my picture, checked my ID, and then sent me on my way. No problem getting through except the struggle I was having with my overweight bag.

What a relief it was to set that bag down. Red came back with food as I was pulling out some of the contents. We had been told by nurses to make sure we ate and drank and, if possible, to rest. I did manage to eat yogurt with fruit a couple of times and get coffee into me every three hours. I managed to get some water in at times, too.

It was already 8:30 p.m. Had the results from the second MRI come back? No, good, I hadn't missed the doctor because of having to leave the hospital. I stayed mostly with Red at this time. He worked on eating his food, and I had gone to get another coffee and was sipping that. We talked some, but mostly we waited.

It was around 10:00 p.m. when the doctor came in to talk with us. It was difficult to concentrate and digest all he was explaining to us. Results: Chris's brain was slowing with the bleeding. Chris's brain showed lots of damage. Even if Chris did survive, he would never be the same. Chris's brain continued to swell. The only hope to relieve pressure from the brain was to remove the skull on the left side. This wouldn't guarantee anything. Chris's brain was damaged, and he would never be the same.

The brain is the only part of our body that when its cells die, they don't repair themselves, nor do new cells take their place. Chris's brain had dead spots all over that totaled to almost half his brain, with most of the damage in the upper left portion. Chris would never be the same even if he were to survive. Chris wasn't going to make it.

It was confusing. At a certain point we knew Chris wasn't going to make it but hoped anyway. We heard about the MRI results but hoped anyway. Heard he'd never be the same but hoped anyway. Heard "even if he were to survive" but hoped anyway, all the while knowing he wasn't going to survive. Hoping he would anyway, knowing it would take an outright miracle. The doctors explained the facts and performed the skull removal; still no changes. Is this the part where they give you time to realize the truth of the matter?

We waited together while they worked on Chris. It was during that time we discussed two important issues. Red brought up the issue of calling Chris's biological mother. After years of no contact, he didn't want to but knew it was what God would want, being she gave birth to Chris, and that he should do it anyway. I tried not to let my personal thoughts scream out at this point. Instead, I chose to give Red a rationalized opinion on how I thought it should be handled. I explained it was 9:00 at night, so why call her and upset her? Then, she wouldn't get a good night's sleep if she could even sleep at all. So that being said, I believe Red thought it best to wait. He never did say one way or another that I remember.

Our second topic of discussion was brought up by me. I don't know why, but it just came out of my mouth. "I think we need to think about something about Chris. I don't want to talk about it, but I think it's important that we make it a decision. I think we really need to decide if we would want Chris to be an organ donor."

"Yeah, I know."

"I can't remember what he decided when he got his license. I think it would be important that he could help others." Red says other things.

It was decided that Chris would be an organ donor. I hoped Chris would forgive us. I didn't want him to ever think we thought of him like a science project. I was thinking of who he could help, the lives he would touch. The children's grandmother being a recipient of a liver, I believe, reminded Red this was a good decision.

Operation completed. Chris's brain continued to swell. More brain damage, dead cells everywhere. We knew what was to come. Standing in the face of truth. Still, we waited. I went to Chris. I sat, I talked to Chris, I cried, and I held his hand before taking another trip to the bathroom.

Before returning to the ICU, I decided to go get yogurt and coffee. I returned to the ICU about 20 minutes later. Upon my return, I heard the sound of the machine beeping, warning the nurse on duty to replace the medicine bag. I stood at Chris's right side and watched as she hurried to attach the new bag.

She didn't make it.

The vital sign machine read flat lines within microseconds. The nurse attached the new bag, and again within seconds, the heartbeat line awakened. The nurse backed away and went to her table without a word or a glance toward me. It only confirmed my worst fears, my deepest sorrows, and the reality of God's plan: Chris was only being kept alive by machines.

We knew this. I didn't mention it.

I went around the bed, sat and ate my yogurt, sipped my coffee, and eventually talked to the nurse. I told her Red and I had decided we wanted Chris to be an organ donor and if she would tell whoever was in charge of that that we'd like to talk to them. She informed me that they had already been contacted and were on standby.

"Oh," was all I could muster.

"But I'll let them know you'd like to speak with them."

Really? Wow! Was that the moment they had been waiting for? Our realization, us knowing for sure Chris wasn't going to make it? I believe she complimented us for thinking of others in our despair. We wanted Chris back! Our truth was God's plan, not our own.

I sat back down and wept. I tried to force myself to sleep. For an hour, I thought I might have. Stay calm, let God lead you. I went to check on Red. He was sleeping in the waiting room. He was so tired. I felt bad in my heart for him. I wanted to make Chris all better for him. I wanted to take away his heartache. I left him sleeping and went back to Chris. I just wanted to be near Chris. I wanted him to know we were there and that I didn't want him to be alone.

Saturday became Sunday. Things began to awaken and become busy in the ICU. I didn't want things to move forward. I knew they'd be coming to speak with us about the organ donor stuff, but they said they'd take Chris off his meds to see if he'd wake up. Or did they already do that? Whatever it was, I know Chris never woke up, and after five hours they put him back on it. When Chris was off the meds, it caused his blood pressure to rise. They believed even though he wasn't awake, at some level his body could feel the pain of all his injuries. Go figure; that part of the brain registered, but he couldn't wake up. So for his humanity's sake, back on the meds he went, and back down the blood pressure went.

When he didn't wake up, we knew it was a rock solid decision that Chris was coming off the machines. After all, ringing in our heads, "Even if Chris was to survive, he'd never be the same." We knew Chris wouldn't want to be bedridden. No way, no how! That was something we knew for sure.

The gentleman in charge of the organ donation took us out of the room to discuss the organ donor matter. He did a wonderful and gentle job explaining everything. Poor Red had to sign all the papers. Almost insulting, but that was Satan trying to weaken me. In this moment, I had to shake my head to stay focused; I was exhausted. I was glad Red had gotten some sleep before this moment. It felt forever long, but Chris had his oldest sister in with him so he wasn't alone. Everything we could possibly give of Chris we did. It was only his body. We hold on fast to our faith knowing "absent from the body, present with the

Lord." We would allow whatever we could to help others, and Chris did that for many. Was it easy? No. Did we think it best? Yes.

So it was done. Monday at 2:30 p.m., Chris would be taken off the machines. Lump in throat, choking tears down, holding it together; remembering all the while this is God's plan. This is God's plan, this is God's plan, this is God's plan...breathe. Not much time left. I want to be near Chris.

Sunday was spent with lots of people showing up. People in Chris's room, the waiting room, phone calls to make. All day long, prayers, tears. Couldn't forget to eat. Visiting with people, consoling others. Be strong, be calm, stay in God's word. Push the feelings aside, and be what God wants you to be.

As evening approached, we realized we had to get the children. As much as we knew we wanted to be near Chris, we also knew we had the responsibility of our other three children. We needed to get to them and explain what was happening. I wanted deep in my heart to stay with Chris but knew Red needed me. I didn't want him to make the hour drive back home alone. I didn't want him to tell the children alone. We needed sleep or at least rest. It killed me, but I chose to stand by my husband knowing Chris was well taken care of by the nurses. I wanted Red to know we were in this together. Therefore, together we stayed. I went to Chris's bedside and took his hand in mine and explained to him why I had to leave and that I would be back as soon as I could. I kissed him on his forehead and hated myself for leaving his side.

Everyone made it home one way or another. Red asked all the children to have a seat on the couch. His oldest sister sat herself nearby on the floor while her boyfriend sat at a distance in the dining room. Red stood while he explained Chris's condition to the children. Because of those conditions, he went on to explain, Chris wasn't going to make it. I sat there numb and exhausted, wanting to move but unable to make myself. It was quiet, tears flowed, and a few questions were asked. It was quiet, and I couldn't take away their pain, nor can I ever. God will have to handle that one. After awhile, it was decided that we would all go our separate ways and try to get some rest so that we could all get back to the hospital early the next morning.

I climbed into my bed feeling guilty that I found comfort in the familiarity of it. Something so routine felt so wrong to be doing. My mind remained on Chris as I laid there. I didn't want to be in bed; I wanted to be sitting at Chris's bedside instead. At some point, I drifted off into a dreamless sleep. I awoke a few hours later in the wee morning hours. I laid there trying not to wake Red. About an hour had passed, and I just couldn't take lying there any longer. I rose to use the bathroom and in doing so woke Red. I told him I wanted to get back to the hospital and be near Chris. We woke the children and were all dressed and heading out the door by 4:30 a.m.

It was Monday, October 3rd, 2011. This day was a day that God knew I'd be leaning on Him 100%, a day where you would see only one set of footprints in the sand.

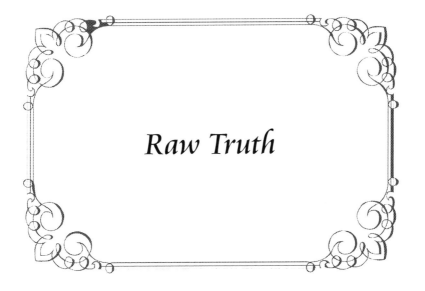

Raw Truth

We went to the hospital and went to our usual waiting room that we had adopted. The children settled in, and I only remember getting to Chris's bedside as soon as I could. I took his hand. I always tried to hold his left hand being he was left-handed. I apologized to Chris for having to leave him and how guilty it made me feel.

I talked to Chris. I knew time was limited this day. Today was the day we would take him off the life support. Today would be the day for all the lasts. The last time I'd hold his hand, the last time I'd see his face, the last time I'd kiss his forehead, the last time I'd sing him a song, the last time I'd whisper softly in his ear, the last time I'd stroke his eyebrow, the last time to touch or see him at all. I just wanted to make time stop.

Couldn't this be one of those times when God would just cast down a heavenly lightning bolt and strike Chris alive? Couldn't it be a moment when I am so overcome with the Holy Spirit that I could demand Chris to awaken and rise up off the bed and he would? Couldn't he just shock the world and wake up and wonder what all the fuss was about? Couldn't he, please God, just this one time, please God? I'm sorry, not this time. God had a different plan He was working on. Even knowing that this raw truth was God's truth didn't ease any emotion.

People came in a lot that day, too, knowing they were coming in to say their goodbyes. Kids from school, people from our church and previously attended church. Our former pastor and his wife came. They stayed with us right up until Red and I went in alone with Chris. We all talked around Chris's bed. We laughed some and cried, too. The beeping machines filled in the blank spots for us.

At one point when the pastor was in the room, Red's oldest daughter was in the room. It had finally occurred to me that after many years, one of my prayers was answered. Crazy how thoughts come to us at odd moments. I had tried to figure many times on my own how I could get the pastor and Red's daughter in the same room. I knew for sure he would lead her to Jesus. It became a prayer of mine that someday this would happen. That time was clearly sitting in front of me. I wasn't about to let it get away from me. God made it clear now it was time to act.

"You know, it has always been a prayer of mine that someday I would get you in the same room as our pastor. We know that Christopher is with Jesus. You know, if you want to see him again, it can happen. All you have to do is accept Jesus as your Lord and Savior."

Then our pastor took over, which I have to admit was a relief. She looked everywhere but at him and fiddled with nearby objects. Truly, she was uncomfortable. Some quiet time passed, and then I stood up and leaned close to her. I asked her if she wanted to pray to Jesus with the pastor. She was crying but managed to say she wanted to do it alone with Chris. Thank you, Lord! We all left the room, and she came out after she prayed. Glory to God! He put us all there in that room at that moment. I thank you God for giving me boldness in that trying moment when you spoke to me. I am joyful knowing that she will see Christopher again!

While good things like this were happening, I still was having resentful feelings within my heart. How could it be that I was standing firm in my faith with everything but this one subject? Chris's girlfriend. Every time someone mentioned her name or someone on "their" side came to check in on Christopher's progress or I saw Red talking to the stepfather, my blood would boil. Just back off! Chris is our son. Not yours! Man 'ole mighty, you've known him a few short weeks, and I've been raising him for 10 years. Go away! Truly not a godly moment.

It also didn't help me that our other two sons were making trips up to visit this girlfriend. They'd come back with, "She said this. She said that. Blah, blah, blah." Part of me was wishing they'd shut up about her already. Why was I behaving like this? I couldn't figure it out until later in the day. The clarity of the lesson hit me like a ton of bricks.

After taking a break from reading my favorite author's work all summer, I had been watching her teach on her new book. The entire weekend, I had managed to use her teachings to help me through this situation with Chris.

Everything but the girlfriend issue.

I was angry at this girlfriend and couldn't figure out why. I knew this was an accident; I knew she wasn't to blame. Her visit earlier in the day to see Chris didn't help the feelings, either.

Red popped his head in the room. "Amber, can I ask you something? Come out here so I can talk to you."

"I don't want to leave Chris."

"It will only take a minute."

I took a deep breath and stepped out into the hallway. "What?"

"The girlfriend's family wants to come and see Chris."

I felt myself turn hot.

"She wants to say her goodbyes."

After wild thoughts flashing through my mind, I agreed, but with the assumption that I wasn't leaving the room. I tried to put myself in her 17-year-old shoes. Puppy love, losing a boyfriend. I knew it would be what Chris would want. Chris is who I did it for. I returned to Chris' side. I wasn't comfortable about seeing the family at all. I had never even seen this girl in my life; she was nothing but a stranger to me.

They arrived. The girlfriend was brought in a wheel chair, her right arm in a cast.

Bam! Not even a chance to look this girl in the eye and the family not even up to the side of Chris's bed when her mother says, "Amber, do you mind if we have a private moment with Chris?"

I'm telling you, I wanted to jump across Chris and scratch her eyes out and scream, "Who in the world do you think you are? What is your major malfunction, woman? Do you even have an ounce of couth within your being?" I was raging inside! On the outside though…

"You've got five minutes." That was all I could muster, but I'm sure my face said more. I marched straight out to Red. Boy was I mad! I thought we had an agreement. I felt betrayed. I felt like a fool. I got suckered.

I talked to Red—about what, I don't know. I talked. I kept thinking this would be okay with Chris. This would be what Chris would want. Just cool it, cool it! Cool it already!

I saw the girlfriend's biological father approaching us. Somehow, I liked him. I felt relaxed with him. He spoke with Red and me and was totally upset. What was wrong? He told us that he wanted to tell Chris "thank you." For what? For Christopher grabbing his daughter and shoving her down into his right side before they struck the pine tree. He had saved her life!

I remembered the injury to Chris's right elbow. He'd gotten his arm smashed into the dashboard because he had wrapped his arm around her. So like Chris to protect those he cared about.

Calm. The calm was coming back in a rush. Calm because I was glad this girl was seeing Chris. Having that moment to say her goodbye. Five minutes had long passed. It didn't seem all that important anymore. In that moment, she rolled out crying. Her father went to her. She thanked me for her visit as she passed by me. I hurried in back to Chris.

I was glad to be alone with Chris again. I was glad the girlfriend had her moment but also glad the moment had passed and that her family was gone. "Don't come back, either!" I wanted to shout to them. I asked God to please tell me what my problem was with this, but at the same time I didn't care just then. I just wanted to be near Chris. Everything else could wait.

Time was growing short, and I only wanted to hold Chris's hand. I saw the clock. I knew the reality. Were we making the right choice? God, will you pull off that miracle? I told myself to stop being foolish. Get a grip! Hold onto your faith tightly! Woman, why do you cry?

My head was whirling, and my feelings were all over the map. In came the nurse, who introduced me to a woman who took care of what they called a "memory box." A what? A memory box? It was explained to me that they take hand prints and hair clippings and whatever else you can think of to put in the box. It was really a nice, unexpected idea.

The three of us all chuckled our way through a number of hand prints. I gave Chris his last haircut. Not an easy task being it looked like he had just gotten one recently. Just the same, I tucked his hair into a small envelope for safe keeping. At one point, I noticed a pile of heart-shaped river rocks someone had placed on Chris's bed. The nurse picked them up one at a time and held them in Chris's right hand. She explained that they would be a gift to each member of the family. After the nurse left, I took each rock myself and held them tightly in his left hand. After all, he was a lefty, and that would be natural.

After Chris had held each rock, I sat there carefully examining each one. They were all different colors with the exception of two. It was decided those two would be for his two brothers. Now Red's, mine, his older sister's, and Priscilla's. I became puzzled when I realized there was an extra river stone. I looked it over carefully, wondering all the while who God had intended me to give this rock to. Like a gentle breeze, all thoughts were of the girlfriend. Everything about that entire situation came into focus. Every verse I'd ever heard and my favorite author saying to "live beyond your feelings" all made sense. In my realization, I was fully overcome with peace. It happened so quickly; it was as if the negative feelings had never existed.

I understood it now! God was allowing me to hold firm to my faith and to focus on Him in this raging storm of Chris' situation. With the girlfriend, it was a real separate emotional moment so I would understand what God was trying to teach me. Choice. He was trying to teach me that living beyond my feelings was a choice. Regardless of my feelings, I had to step out of them, to totally acknowledge what I wasn't able to do myself and let God do it for me, to forget what I felt and to do what is right in God's eyes just the same. I made that choice right in that moment! I was up and on my feet on my way to the waiting room.

"Red, bring me up to Chris's girlfriend's room."

Red looked at me bewildered. "What? Okay."

"Right now."

Red walked, and I followed. Down the hall, up the elevator around more halls, people were everywhere. Now I was the one asking for a private moment alone.

Here came the father. I could tell everyone was shocked I was there. After all, I mean really. Red told the father I'd like to speak with his daughter if that would be okay. He said he would go ask her. We waited outside in the hallway while people glanced our way. It felt uncomfortable, but I didn't care.

I got the go-ahead from his daughter to go on in. Thank you, God. I had to work this out with her. At this point, I realized Satan was trying to put a wedge in between us and using me to do the dirty work. We talked, and I made amends with her. During our conversation, I gave her the extra heart-shaped river rock. She cried as I explained to her why she was getting that gift. We hugged, and the Devil lost again. All that drama to learn a lesson of choice. My goodness, that was stressful to say the least. I went back to Chris.

At Chris's side holding his hand, I wanted to say so much. I knew time was short. It was hard to find the words. I knew though that it truly didn't matter because soon enough he'd be in Heaven, and maybe he could hear me then. I told him I was sorry I didn't hold his hand more often when he lived at home and I should've hugged him more often. I wish our time together wasn't so stubborn. I looked forward to Chris having his own place, under his own roof, so we would be able to spend time enjoying each other as individuals instead of rules and "who's the boss" all the time. Then I could mess up his house, eat his food, and vent about his brothers in his space. I looked forward to going shopping for stuff for him, gifts for the kitchen and blankets and, well, just stuff. I know it would've driven him nuts, but I would've done it just the same.

Now, there would be nothing, nothing except lessons from the past that God gave me to learn and now live by. God used Chris to grow me, while all the while I thought I was growing Chris for the world. God's plan was not ours. I missed Chris when he left home those first few weeks but hey, what the heck, I'd call him sometime when I felt it was right and bug him then. We always think we have tomorrow, don't we?

What were those nurses doing now? Things were being taken away; the neck brace was removed. The clock read 1:30 p.m.; there was only an hour left. They were preparing Chris's departure. Time was drawing near. I had to warn everyone.

I went to the waiting room and told the children that they needed to come in and see Chris. They came back with me to Chris's room to say their last goodbyes. One by one, they are asked if they would like to take Chris by his hand. David declined and stayed put at the doorway. I took Bradley's hand together with mine and placed it into Chris's.

I spoke to Bradley softly in his ear. "Don't cry baby, please don't cry. We'll see him again. Hold on to that. We will see him again."

Priscilla took Chris's hand with mine, and her tears began to fall. I held her and stroked her hair and knew this was something only God could fix. I whispered softly in her ear until she was ready to let go.

No dry eyes and a numb silence as I had the pastor and his wife and Red take the children back to the waiting room. I waited alone with Chris for their return. I held Chris's hand knowing all too well that soon he'd be gone, and I'd be unable to hold him anymore.

Red returned from the waiting room and shortly after was followed by the pastor and his wife. They had wheeled Chris away by then, and it gave me and Red a time alone to say goodbye but not our last.

The organ donor man led the four of us off to a different location in the hospital, where they would be carrying out the last moments of Chris's journey here on Earth with us. It seemed like a long walk, and my feet were heavy and not wanting to be moving forward. We arrived at the entrance of another hallway, where Red and I changed into some blue scrubs. We pulled them over our own clothes.

I don't want to do this. We have to. I don't want Chris to go away. He already is.

After dressing, we left the pastor and his wife to wait for us at that location. I wanted them to be there because I had no idea what was about to happen or how I would react. If need be, I wanted the pastor's wife to take care of me.

We were led to Chris' side for our final moments with him. All tubes had been removed already. We were told his hand would be uncovered so we could hold it, but it wasn't. I stood next to Chris, no tubes, no beeping machines, nothing.

But wait! He was breathing! I saw his chest moving up and down on its own. I turned to Red. I turned back to Chris. I stroked Chris's face. I looked at the doctors. His heart was strong, they told us, as if assuring me it wouldn't last. It didn't.

Slower his chest moved. Slower, slower, slower. I couldn't feel his breath passing out his nostrils any longer. The doctor stepped forward. A tear rolled down my check. The doctor shook his head no.

We had already been warned the doctors only had five minutes to get Chris's organs once the heart stopped beating. We did not want to interfere with the lives of others that Chris was about to save. Quick, one last goodbye. I stepped away so that Red could go to Chris's side a little closer. I watched him say goodbye to Chris, and my heart ached for him. We walked together as we were once again led back to where we had only minutes before prepared for this moment.

We had been warned to be prepared for the worst. We were told some people moan or thrash around and other behaviors like that when they get removed from the machines. Not Chris; gently, away he slipped off into God's kingdom quietly; no nightmare to fight off now. Thank you, God, thank you for taking him so gently.

It was Monday, October 3rd, 2011 at 3:28 p.m. Chris was with Jesus! I was calm. We all walked back to the waiting room. The nurse ended up by my side as we went along our way. Where were the pastor and his wife? How did Red get separated from me? The nurse was talking to me, telling me how strong we were. She could see we truly loved each other, never had she seen a couple so caring toward each other, putting always the other's needs first. I told her thanks, but in my mind, I was thinking how sad it must be for other couples when that is only what God expects from us in our relationship. I just wanted to find Red.

I departed from the nurse at some point and found my way back to the waiting room. There were so many people there. Now everyone knew; Chris wasn't with us any longer. We all talked awhile. We formed a circle and prayed. More tears and hugs. People started departing.

We gathered together, all of us, only five now. We got our belongings and headed down the hallway. It was time to leave. I was thinking how you've got to be kidding; I mean really, that's it? We just pack our things and go home? God, this couldn't be it!

It *is* it. Chris is gone, gone to be with Jesus, and it still doesn't seem real to me. I miss you Chris! I do. I miss you and wish for you to come pulling up in the driveway with your ugly truck to bust my chops. I do miss you, but I know for true 100% that God has a plan, and you fulfilled yours here. Be it painful or not, that is the way it is. I know you are with the Lord, and I am pleased knowing you are in no pain or sorrow. I know your heart isn't angry anymore. I had prayed that often for you, Chris, but never ever did I think it would be answered like this. I miss you and wonder often what you are doing up there in God's kingdom. You're such a brat, getting out of so much that happens down here in this world. No headaches, no working, no bills, no taxes, no freezing work days. None of it! No dirty diapers, no nagging wife, no broken down cars. No, not you. We'll just skip all that and get the grand prize. Jesus! Being with Him! I can't wait to be there, too, to be able to see you again, and maybe you can give me a big bear hug. I love you, Chris, and I'll do my best to do it God's way.

It's Official

It has been fifteen months now since that last walk out of Eastern Maine Medical. Fifteen months and counting. A circumstance you don't ever seem to stop the counting. A circumstance that will always remain the same and will never change until I see our son again.

I have purposely waited these past months to continue with you on my walk. The walk I have dedicated to our God. How was I to know what the next year would bring. I only knew that I had the official one year of mourning in front of me. At this point I had decided only two things, one was to do it with as much grace as I could and second without denying my emotions. I refused to let any of it draw me into a depression. I had a choice to make and I chose to take care of business all the while leaning on God.

One thing I have learned through this is that life doesn't stop. Regardless, of what I was going through the world around me was still moving forward. At first it was unbearable. I wanted to shout to the world, STOP! Can't you see I'm hurting over here! Don't you even care my son just died? Is what you have going on so important that you can't even take a minute to share in my pain? No, people don't and by no fault of their own. People aren't mind readers. All they are going to see is what is upon my face. Then they will draw their own conclusions if they were even to give it any thought. This pain is my own.

I was thankful for the friends I had and the ones who were willing to be there for me. We can't expect everyone's life to change just because ours has. We have to walk through our trials, knowing that we are not alone but will carry the burden. How we walk through it is ultimately on our shoulders. I came to that place where it was time for another major decision. That choice was mine to make. I could walk through this trial letting the pain control me or taking that pain and letting God use it for His glory. My choice, as difficult as it may be, is to let God use me and the trial for His glory. Here I am, God.

My mind whirls with so much information that I want to share with you. I'm nervous and excited all at once. My chest still remains tightened while my fingers try to find the correct letters on the key board to form into words. Words that have meaning and lead you on this journey with me. Pain is fresh once again from reopening the wound. I've had to read what I wrote to you a year ago to get some sort of bearing on how to proceed on this walk with you again. You have become a friend that I need to catch up with. Someone I'm rawly truthful with. A best friend, even, because I don't skim the minor details off the top. I go deep into my heart to reach yours and to open you up to the truth within me. Each vulnerable step I take is all with Gods leading. Losing Christopher has left a hole in everyone's life that has known him. It is a space that can never be filled with anything or anyone else. It was Chris' space to fill, his life to live and now that life here on earth has ended. The only parts to that story that remain is how each of us continue with our lives. I had a bit of a rocky start with mine but this journey God has set my course on has continued to grow.

It wasn't until I came home form the hospital that Oct.3rd, 2011 evening that my exhaustion hit me like a ton of bricks. That was a Monday and still I couldn't just collapse onto the bed and sleep away my pain. After all, I had to cook dinner. How could these children possibly be hungry at a time as this. But they were and I had to get something onto the table, get showers taken care of and get them into bed so they could go to school Tuesday morning. School? Yes school. While in the hospital we were told by one of the nurses to maintain as much normalcy as possible. So we asked the children if they wanted to stay home or go to school the next day and they all wanted to go to school. So be it. I just wanted to crawl under my blanket and pretend this wasn't happening and they wanted to journey away form the house. I thought it would be good for them to be surrounded by everyone to give them support. So Red and I agreed if that was what they wanted then let them go.

Meanwhile, we would stay at home and prepare for the funeral arrangements. The funeral would be held on that Saturday the 8th. It was arranged that we would have the service at the gym at Fox-Croft Academy so that all the high school could attend. We also informed all our church family and of course various papers had the obituary. Red spent hours preparing a dvd with music and pictures of Chris only to have it crash on Friday late in the afternoon. Again, my heart ached for him and there was nothing I could do to fix it. He managed to get another dvd together but it wasn't nearly as lovely as the first one.

I had told God right form the beginning back in September of 2011 that when He purposely got my attention that I would be ready and told Him in prayer that I would do things His way. Saying and doing are two different things which isn't any new revelation to the world. My first lesson was the one back in the hospital about learning to do things even if you weren't feeling like it. Well, those lessons came one after another that first week while preparing for the Chris's funeral.

Our first morning at home consisted of getting the children off to school and then off to our appointment at the local funeral home. That was a difficult walk into their doors. While taking each step I replayed a scenario that took place in our vehicle while passing the funeral home on our way by it to head home. It was a Sunday after church not more then a month before and Chris had made some wisecrack about the service taking place. I snapped a remark back at him about being rude and how would he like it if it was his funeral. Now here I was, knowing exactly how it felt.

I tried to stay emotionally under control while working out the details of the funeral by just being all business. Red remained calm and courteous and I was tense and demanding on the verge of being borderline rude. I was choking bac k the lump in my throat all the while. I did try to be polite and was so thankful that the young man in charge was familiar with all types of grief stricken behaviors. The only incident that brought tears to my eyes was when we were asked if we would pay for the bill in one lump sum or would we prefer monthly payments. I expressed there was no way that I wanted to go to the mailbox each month to be reminded of this event. This was even taken into consideration a short while after when they needed to send us a small refund. I was so thankful for this consideration that I told them to just go ahead and mail it. The phone call gave me the strength I needed to see that envelope in our mailbox. That is God taking care of me again. He knows my weaknesses.

It has dawned on me in the past months also, yes, God knows all of me. Every thought every action every motive; all of me. That is why He thought ahead to warn me that something was going to happen in my life that I needed to be ready for. I wasn't warned to be ready because I was having some angelic breakthrough with the spiritual world or God was asking me to go out and do some extraordinary works for Him. No! I believe God warned me out of His love for me and out of my weakness. I was being sent the biggest trial of my lifetime and I was going to have to hold onto all my faith. Please know, far be it for me to even begin to think what God's motive was. I have only been thankful for whatever His reason and that true reason is only for Him to know and for us to give him the praise and glory through it. It is in being human that I pondered the situation and try to find a lesson in it. I remain thankful that I did receive a warning and thankful that I became aware that there was even something going on around me. I can't even begin to think how things would have played out without it. It just reinforces to me that I matter to God.

Another challenge that was needed to be face was calling Chris's biological mother. This wasn't my direct responsibility but I needed to give my support to my husband. We for no other reason wanted to make the phone call other then out of common courtesy. We also knew that this is what God would of wanted us to do. I know that sounds harsh but she hadn't seen the

children for over eight years. There are personal issues there and not for me to be talking about but the bottom line remains the same. There had been no contact for years. Still the phone call had to be made.

Red had hunted down her phone number and called her. I think he asked her if she was home. She had confirmed that she was so he gave her the tragic news concerning Chris's death. I could hear her through the phone. All the questions. I felt bad in my heart for her. There she was probably all by herself and to get an unexpected phone call with such horrible news. I had hoped she was able to get someone to come over to be with her if needed.

I had spoken to Red at the hospital about calling her. I remember him taking my advise not calling her late into the evening as it was. At some other point we discussed waiting to tell her once we knew for sure that Chris was going to be taken off of the life support. We discussed that it would be pointless for her to come to the hospital and have to drive over three hundred miles in an emotional condition. Red decided to wait and that phone call came on Tuesday morning Oct.4th hoping she would be told before someone else informed her.

At the hospital there was a lot of news flying around on facebook. It became somewhat annoying to have people telling each other things and at some of those times being inaccurate. Even the news stations had information that they were reporting. It all just felt like an invasion of privacy.

Once the initial phone call was made to Chris's biological mother the next issue arose. She understandably wanted to attend the funeral. We had mixed feelings about this. On one hand we understood completely that she had given birth to this child. On the other hand, we needed to take into consideration the other three children. They had not seen their biological mother for such a long time that one child had no interest in seeing her, one hardly remembers her and the third doesn't remember her at all. She is a complete stranger to them. When it was all said and done the result of the decision was that she could attend the funeral under one condition, that she was not to approach the children. Again, you may think this harsh. It was our intention to protect the children from any further emotional upset. She unfortunately, did not keep her side of the agreement.

Red and I along with Priscilla and David were seated in the front row waiting for the proceeding to begin. Red was addressed by someone and had to leave his seat momentarily. Bam! Like a flock of seagulls, not only did she approach us but the entire group of family members that had accompanied her to Maine. It was horrible! She and myself were the only ones that knew what was happening. I was so numb from everything that was happening in my life that I just sat there. I just couldn't believe how selfish it all seemed to me. She got her reward though. One that will be with me and probably her for the rest of our lives. Upon bending in front of Priscilla she hesitated and asked Priscilla would it be okay to hug her. Priscilla's response still tears at my heart. She said, "I don't know who you are, but I guess it's okay." As she released Priscilla from the hug she proclaimed," I'm your mom." It saddens me that this is the way Priscilla was introduced to her biological mother. None the less, on the day of her brothers funeral. David greeted her with a hug and Bradley never recognized her even when he had been only a couple of feet away from her.

At the end of the service we had been directed on where to stand as all guests departed. However, to avoid any further contact with Chris's biological mother Red whispered to me to stay put and let people come to us in a round about way. This must of really confused the funeral director. It turned out well for others though. For those who chose to come through the line to give condolences did and others where free to go. I kept Priscilla by my side and David within eye sight until we were comfortable that we were not going to be invaded again. I eventually let Priscilla go off with our kind hearted neighbors who would bring her home for us. After only a scant amount of people remained did Red and I also chose to leave.

Red carried out Chris's urn and I had some balloons that someone had given Chris at the hospital. I had set up eight by ten picture frames containing pictures of Chris from birth all throughout his school years. I had placed a wooden cross between the years he lived without Christ and the year he received Christ. I wanted to make a point that we never know when God is going to take us and that we need to make a decision to chose Jesus before it is to late. Chris had five years left after his decision.

Somehow all these items at the funeral all ended up back at home. All but the balloons. When Red and I went outside I released them into the wind. We watched as they lifted into the autumn blue sky and walked away as they got out of sight. We returned home amongst our friends. You'd think I'd add to that phrase, family, but that was hardly the case. Only my sister, Melonie and her boyfriend went home with us afterward. I wanted everyone to come back to our place but each one had a long drive back to their own homes with their awaited responsibilities.

Our reception came and went with a blur. People were already on their way out even before I was able to sit down and try to get something into my stomach. Our church friends came from each church but who exactly I wouldn't be able to name. Melonie sat next to me while I picked at my food and was still there after everyone else departed. I hated to see her leave but they had at least a six hour drive ahead of them. Besides, Joe, had to get back to work come Monday and would need that Sunday to get himself rested physically and mentally to face that workday. Wouldn't we all. Death never comes at a convenient time does it? All things are in Gods timing and if He says "now" then that time is best. Keep your emotions at bay and you'll see things more clearly but never quite able to grasp completely Gods plan. This is okay with me; it even gives me an inner peace and the ability to remain calm.

Our Sunday morning wouldn't find rest there either. We attended our church service. Our hearts were saddened but we still love our God. To be with our church family and worship our Lord was what we wanted. Being with our church family was going to continue after church service; being followed by a wedding. We had excepted the invitation and wanted to attend; the timing was just off for us emotionally. We put our feelings on the back burner and shared in their happiness.

This wasn't our "first after the funeral" outing though. We had time between the church service and the wedding so Red with his usual way of finding something to do to fill the gap brought us to a local corn maze. Red and I stayed together and the children ran off by themselves to enjoy their adventure through the corn. It was a fun time for all but my mind couldn't help wander to thoughts of Chris enjoying being there with us. I wondered if he had thought to bring a date here to enjoy the seasonal fun. Or maybe he would of thought it to "corny".

Before we departed we purchased a pumpkin for each of us. By seasons end they would all be carved and put out on display on the front steps. I had also asked Red if I could get a t-shirt to remember this day by, something I don't usually do.

As we drove out to head for the wedding my thoughts kept going back to Chris and him not being with us to enjoy the day. The day was bright and sunny without a cloud in the sky. Perfect autumn air to breath, it was just so nice. Then there it was as if to say "everything is going to be all right"; a big puffy heart shaped cloud. No where else in the sky was anything; just blue skies and the big puffy cloud. Chris knows I like the heart shape and I couldn't help believing that he was trying to reach out to me at that moment. It brought tears to my eyes and a smile to my face knowing still that he was trying to take care of me.

Mourning Walk

Tomorrow getting back to the game of life will be upon all of us. I don't want to face this but it is the way it is. I want to be alone in my own thoughts but life would have it that this week we will be getting a new roof put on our home. Nothing quiet about this. I suppose it was a needed distraction in one way or another. Distracting it was, too. Thump, thump, thump. Bang, bang, bang and by the fourth day it was completed. I was glad to get my privacy back.

After that first week, I was able to have time to myself. Everything seemed so different. The sky was more blue, birds songs were so clear, the sunshine warmed my skin just right. My world just kept moving around me and somehow I was walking with it. Mindful of my presence in it but feeling on the outside looking in. Numb! Ah yes, I was warned by someone along the way that I would become this way. I really hadn't noticed until I was growing away from the numbness. The world we live in is busy. All that busyness is like a wake-up call saying; hello I need you over here and I need you over here and by the way I need you over here. Yikes, it's no wonder people take so long to "mourn"; they can never seem to have time to get it out of their system. I think it was something I read that first month that in our world exists a country that when a loved one dies they go into their grass hut and only come out getting back to business when they have decided that they are finished mourning. I think that is a great idea! Our world is different though, hurry up and get with the program already! I sometimes wonder how long I would be in that grass hut.

That Oct of 2011 I did things just to keep me busy and other things because I just outright had to. I chose to go out each morning to walk. This was a time that I could just pray and at times talk to Chris; then more often then not I would cry my soul dry. Crisp autumn air and a good cry was therapy for me. By the time I returned home I was able to keep my mind on the things I had to take care of.

I was determined that I would relieve Red of any business pertaining to Chris. Red has a job that needs every bit of his attention in order that no one on the job get injured and I wanted his head to remain in the game. First order of business, was to collect Chris's belongings from the place he was staying and also from the "girlfriends" home. I along with David went and retrieved the items at Chris's place. It was a stressful event. The same boxes he had moved just three weeks before hadn't even been unpacked yet. I sat on his bed and grabbed his blanket and stuffed it into my face just to try and smell him. I cried and tried to stop myself, reminding myself to stay focused at the task at hand. David was the one who carried everything to the car. I packed up the items Chris had thrown everywhere. All those years teaching him to keep his room cleaned up still weren't being practiced. Doesn't matter at all now and mattered to much then.

After everything of Chris's was returned home I had the chore of sorting through it. I gave some of his things to his siblings and most of it I packed away. Some things I even threw away. That was difficult. Try as we may to hold onto someone's possessions to make them nearer to us eventually becomes empty. They are gone and nothing brings them back and nothing makes them closer. Along the way I have given more of Chris's things away as well. I've concluded that I may as well let Chris help out others rather then to have things sit around and collect dust. It makes me happy to think that his blankets or clothing are keeping someone in need warm this winter. Besides, every time I look at his things I would get a big lump in my throat and that just isn't productive. Helping people stay warm or giving away the slightly used work boots and hand me down clothing to Bradley and Priscilla that is what is productive.

I had washed all the clothes and blankets before I bagged them up. That made me cry too. I tired to put off washing all the blankets because I was still stuffing my nose in them when I was alone down in the basement doing my own laundry. Eventually though, his scent faded and I kept telling myself to stop acting like a fruit loop and wash the blankets already! I cried when I let the thoughts of this being his last load of laundry that I would ever wash enter into my mind. I cried when I hung the clothes out to dry on the line for the last time. And I cried when I folded them up and put them away. It's okay to cry, even Jesus wept. Jesus even cried at one of his friends funeral when He knew later that His friend would live again. Really, it's the same for me. I know Chris is alive in heaven and that someday I will see him again. In these moments though, when the wound of loss is still fresh we tend to focus on the loneliness and all the hopes and dreams of the future that will never take place. Expectations.

Ideas and plans suddenly erased from our world filled with a black void. We become changed forever, set on a new course charted only by our heavenly Father. That too, is okay. When I remember who is in control and that all things work by His will I can pull myself together and remain focused. Regardless, of the storm we need to count it all joy. This may take time and our emotions may not be agreeing with us but we know that Jesus is in control. I know, it doesn't always feel good being used. We are tools being used and if we can remember this we can gently place our emotions aside knowing we are doing a work for the Lord. He is unfolding His story through us; sometimes we are the hammer and other times we are the nail.

I eventually, received Chris's last paycheck in the mail. That created a chain of events going back and forth to the bank. The safe that we had given Chris for his birthday became an issue as well. Chris accidently locked his key to the safe inside of the safe along with his wallet. Still to this date we have yet to send off a thirty dollar check to retrieve the new set of keys and combination lock number. With that I should have Chris's chores taken care of. I'm sure another will find a way of sneaking in there even now.

Pain just kept finding its way into my life this Oct. All the while, we were handling the sad events of Chris's I was dealing with another loss. I have mentioned that we had to put our goat Dolly down. I had spent the entire day with Dolly. I dragged her outside in the grass where she could be in the sunshine. A neighbor had come over earlier in the day with the backhoe to dig her grave and I knew my time was limited with her. So I laid out in the grass with her like I used to do with all my goats back in Carroll. Each time I was about to doze off she would baa and I would pop awake. I stayed by her side five straight hours. After the children came home I had Priscilla stay with her. We took some pictures and let her have a bit of grain. Eventually, Red came home and we said our last good-byes. I gave Dolly a handful of raisins and went into the house to be with Priscilla. I held her ears tight while I cried and heard the gunshot ring out.

Who could ever imagine the event of pumpkin season would tear your heart out. Each year, as many of us do, I get a pumpkin for each child. This year I wasn't going to let it be any different. Each child carried their pumpkin off to be carved and little did I know it was going to be another heart tearing moment. The three children had each decided to dedicate their pumpkin to Chris. I blinked away my tears and swallowed back the lump in my throat as I took their picture.

When I wasn't purposely finding something to keep my mind busy I would just sit outside in the grass while my dog ran around. Sitting out in the autumn sunshine is one of my favorite things to do. The sun is warm and the breeze is cool so you have to wear a jacket to keep warm. I just soak it all up. I spent a lot of those times talking to Chris and praying to Jesus. I would cry my eyes out and try to get all the tears out of my system before the children came home form school. I just felt so far away from Chris. I know that when I pray Jesus hears me but was Chris hearing me too? I don't have the answer to that question. I only know what happened to me when I do talk to Jesus and Chris. I was laying out in the grass one day talking and crying when suddenly this sound rang out. What in the world was that? I sat up to see an eagle in our driveway! It cried out once more then took off flying. I'd never seen that eagle in our yard before and still to this day it hasn't been here since. What's the big deal about that? Well, Chris loved eagles. The timing of it just makes me wonder why was that eagle there and from who if anyone. Chris loves eagles, me crying my eyes out for Chris and the timing; I believe somehow Chris was reaching out to me again. What the message was exactly I don't know. I do know it awed me enough to get my attention and stop my crying.

That was October 2011, eleven official months of mourning to go.

NOVEMBER 2011

By now I have already been well into a couple of books that were given to myself and the family. Books that help give you support helping you to make it through your mourning period. Books that help you to grasp what you may be feeling and feelings yet to come. I dove right into these books. I wanted to know if what I was feeling was normal and as I read I became aware that I was.

One of the books was on grief given to me by our former Pastor. Another grief pamphlet was one of a series I would receive throughout the next six months. That one was a gift from the women's Bible study group that I once attended back in CT at Groton Bible Chapel. The third book was about a young boy who went to heaven and spent time their with Jesus. That book got my attention because I wanted to know what it may be like there for Chris. It gave me a great comfort knowing that Chris is in a place surrounded with peace and love. Overall, I enjoyed reading any information that let me know there were people out in the world that knew what I was going through. I was not alone and I could even pick up the phone and call someone if I needed to talk.

In the pamphlet series it eventually came to the point of talking about the holiday's. However, my mourning time didn't fall in order with the pamphlets. Thanksgiving was on the way. My annual routine is to have the house decorated for the autumn season which flows right into the Thanksgiving holiday. This year I only gave it a half hearted attempt.

Red and I had decided that we would have our dinner alone with the children We weren't in the mood to have noise yet and we wanted to use the time off from the daily routine to slow down and catch our breath in a sort of way. Our morning went as usual, preparing our turkey dinner for five. We usually have a table of goodies set up to munch on throughout the day but we didn't have the energy to put any effort into that this year. The children slept in and made sure they were out in the living room snuggled up in their blankets to watch the parade on tv. Finally, we all cleaned up, dressed and sat down for our Thanksgiving dinner. Then bam, like a lighting bolt, there it was. Grief stricken. Coming what seemed out of nowhere. Red said our prayer and then we looked at each other both with tears in our eyes. Even the children choked up. Nothing was said, we all knew what we were feeling, there was no need for words.

I forced my pain down not wanting to upset the children any further. I kept thinking of what might be the reality of the day if Chris was with us. He had been spending a lot of time with his girlfriend and her family so I am sure that would be where he would have had his dinner. We may have gotten a phone call or maybe not. If he had called, I would of bribed him to come over with the blueberry pie I made in remembrance of him. However he would of chose to express his independence would of been fine with me because I knew that is what it would of been about. After all, it was his first holiday to chose what he would of done with it and I am sure that once more he would put his "free will" choice into play.

During the month of November I had more going on then just the holiday. At some time after coming home from the hospital God did not stop working on me. With clear direction I knew He had told me that I should write down my experience of this tragedy about Chris. I say clearly I know this because it is like having no doubt. It was messages I heard on the same subject over and over to the point it was something that stood out. So I'm like, "well, what does this have to do with me?" This message of write this down, write this down was just so clear. So that is what I did. I started writing in my journal. Nothing to difficult, after all, who is ever going to see my journal anyway?

My second project of the month was to put together a testimonial. I was asked to give my testimonial at the up-coming women's annual retreat in Springfield, ME. When asked I did not hesitate to answer yes. I had already decided that if God was going to use me during this tragedy that I would do whatever He asked of me. How could I say no. The subject matter was on obedience to God.

During this time I was able to stay focused on my relationship with Jesus. I knew that this time in my life wasn't to hurt me. God was using it to grow me. To change my character to become more like Jesus. I gave this every bit of my energy because I knew it was all for my own good. If I were to struggle and try to get away from it then God would just use another method to get to me. I chose to embrace the discomfort of change and as I did I was filled with a peace and spiritual fulfillment that only Gods word can give.

I found my study time to be a challenge that I actually enjoyed. I liked learning that God loved me and grew me because of that love. I enjoyed when my questions found answers and my thoughts created even more questions. Puzzle pieces fell into place and lightbulb moments were ever so refreshing. I was thankful for this distraction. A distraction that put my pain into an understanding. I was sorry that I had to put away this project while the children had their break from school.

That was November, 2011; ten official months of mourning to go.

DECEMBER 2011

Could it be, Christmas season upon us already? This meant taking all the autumn decorations down and replacing them with a Christmas wonderland. Taking away things wouldn't take long it was the replacing them part that put a weight on my shoulders. I'm sure some of you may be thinking, "well, why bother." I had to bother. I was trying to "maintain normalcy", remember? Besides, back at the end of October, when I showed a lack of enthusiasm decorating, Priscilla had asked me if we were still going to do our usual Christmas decor. I didn't want to disappoint her regardless of how selfish that it was of her to ask such a question. But she is only a young girl and how is she to know the struggles I was going through. So up the decorations went. Slowly and a little out of my order of things but they did go up. I had the children put the tree up first, which is what I usually do last. Every day I would do a little more until it was completed.

This holiday Red and I chose to have company over. I invited some young men that are family friends. They are brothers that the boys knew from school and the rest of us knew from attending church. I thought they would enjoy the invitation and we would enjoy their company. I knew it was going to be a day that we would need the void of Chris to be filled. We were thankful when they answered our invite with a "yes". As it turned out we all had an enjoyable day filled with lots of noise, great food and laughter. This time when prayer was said we didn't cry and I asked God that if He could would He please tell Chris that we all said "hello".

You would think that with just the busyness of Christmas alone that that would of been enough of a distraction from all my emotions; but no. Challenges continued to be piled on thicker and thicker. I thought how unfair it all seemed. I didn't even get a chance to catch my breath and the darts just kept coming at me. Back in September we were confronted with an issue that involved our other two sons. Unfortunately, it also involved the law. Due to Chris's accident, our son who chose to take all the blame for the unlawful behavior, was able to settle the matter with an amount of restitution. This meant having to forego the drivers ed glass that he was saving for. Hopefully, the sting of the consequence would be enough of a reminder to avoid any future mistakes. Now the only remnant of the situation was the stress that I carried within me.

The children, of course, were back in school come December. That meant for me that I could continue with my studies on obedience to God. It was great to have that focus.

I also had another subject to focus on that I find great enjoyment in doing. That came in the form of Christmas shopping. Instead of joining the crowds in the stores I decided to do most of my Christmas shopping through catalogs and home shopping channels. I wasn't ready yet to be around to many people and memories of shopping with Chris would just flood my mind when I had gone out before. I had already had a meltdown once before in the store that we are a member of. I was loading a fifty pound bag of dog food onto my cart and was having some difficulty with maneuvering it onto the lower rack. This made me think of all the times that Chris would lift the bag for me and it just started a flood of tears. I was thankful that there wasn't anyone in the isle with me as I tried to get myself back in control. I fought with these emotions throughout the entire shopping experience. Finally, outside the store on my way to the car I just couldn't keep it inside any longer and all the tears just burst forth. Wouldn't you know it, of all the times I've been in and out of that parking lot this was the day someone parked right next to me decides to be friendly and make some small talk. A comment on the amount of groceries I had purchased. With hardly a glance I gave him a reply about that's how it is with three growing teenagers. With my head down I hurried along emptying the groceries into the back of my car. I couldn't seem to get in my car fast enough and when I finally settled into the drivers seat I sat there until I could dry my eyes. I didn't care if the car next to me had not decided to pull away. In fact, I didn't care about anything in that moment. I was crying and I knew why and when I was past this I would move on, until then I was in my own world of pain. It took about fifteen minutes before I was able to get the crying out of my system and know that I was in the frame of mind to drive my car safely.

My shopping was just going to be a little different this year is all. It became routine for me to get my cup of coffee, sit on the coach and after my morning devotions on went the tv. I had fun seeing all the different items presented and trying to decide what would be the smartest gift for each one on my shopping list. I had a list but I also had a budget. This fun counteracted the stresses that still continued to grow in my life.

I know right well that the Bible tells us that God will not give us more then we can handle, that He is always with us, and if we draw nearer to Him that He will draw nearer to us. So why then do I feel like I'm in a rushing river being threatened to get pulled under at any given moment. One wave after another across my face seeming as if every breath will be my last. Was the trauma of Chris truly not enough to draw me closer to God now having to add all these extras. God, please, you know that I am already on my knees! I'm crying out to You, I'm relying on Your word to get me through! Poof! There it was like a breath across my right cheek; an answer. Surrender all. So I have been learning to give ALL of me to our heavenly Father. Still, I wasn't quite there in that December of 2011. I chose to meet my darts head on as they came my way.

As usual, these darts that came at me were in the form of children's behavioral issues. I may add that these issues did not stem form the loss of Christopher; this has been an on going issue. It was just so frustrating to me that they had to continue. I did my best not to let the emotions I felt from the situations control me. After all, I am only here to watch over these situations as they play themselves out not try to control them. I can only advice the children and try to guide them in better choices but it will be up to them what they do. In the meantime, I had to battle with their actions not dragging me down. Not letting them "steal my joy", as Christian lingo would say.

What I thought they were stealing from me most was my mourning period. It was like not getting any time to deal with what was going on inside me and having to jump right back into life. Nothing ever stops including the children's wrong choices. These choices once again put the law back on my doorstop. Stress! Suspensions from school. Stress! Detentions in school. Stress! Giving ME bad attitudes because the consequences they had to endure. Stress! Red traveling back and forth to work and being here only on the weekends. Stress! Please, God, can I catch a break here? No, not yet. Oh, and by the way, hold on tight, this ride isn't over yet.

Now my alone time was even more limited. During my time alone I could pray and cry and scream Chris's name out loud when I wanted to. I could still pray but my cry was stifled and there was no screaming out Chris's name like I'd do when calling him to dinner. My mourning was being held back once more. It was only while writing in my journal I could find some emotional relief; a place where God was allowing me to empty my grief. God always gives us a way out and I was glad to have my journal or I may have become like a shook bottle of soda waiting to blow its top.

The air I breathed was Gods word. I remained focused on Jesus. I was so thankful that this month we would celebrate His birth. When I allowed this to be the forefront of my thoughts, then it made all of circumstances bearable. I praised God for Jesus and I thanked Jesus for being willing to carry out Gods plan. I thanked God for our pastors sermons and all the wonderful music, the fellowship with other Christians in my life. I soaked in as much love as I could find and tried to find ways to give some back. Christmas cards were going out and coming in and my gifts to give were starting to arrive to be wrapped. Excitement of the holiday was filling the air. God would carry me through this holiday season and that is exactly what He did.

That was December 2011, nine official months of mourning to go.

Happy New Year?

January 2012

With ease we breeze through the holiday season wishing everyone a "Happy New Year". I tried to grasp at that thought and incorporating it into my life but it just wouldn't take hold. Yes, it may turn out to be happy but in the meantime I was just moving from day to day. The fog was lifting but my heart still ached. Knowing we all were moving into a new year and without Chris. A year that we just assumed that he had along with us to live. The calendar would no longer read 2011 it would read 2012. We were moving further and further away from him as each day passed. The season has moved from autumn to winter and soon enough to spring all of which he would have no part in. It all just put my stomach up in a twist. A feeling like getting butterflies. Still my life tugged at me to keep moving on.

With the start of this new year the family vacation had come to an end as well. Left alone to my own thoughts while the children were in school and Red was back to work. The Women's Retreat was just a few short days away and I had to get the final touches on my testimonial. Just a little while longer and this could be put behind me. It's a wonder what one can do when their whole mind is focused. I asked God to please give me whatever it takes to do this work because this would be the longest amount of time I had ever spoke in front of a crowd. I finally got to a point were I could practice and it wasn't a matter of having to add more to my time it was a matter of having to shorten the amount of time. How was I going to do that? After all, what does one think more important in one's life then another to put the point across to people that at one time I actually outright told God "no" to reaching a place in my life when I say to God, "Here I am Lord". So instead of making any cuts I just decided to "chance it". So that was that and I left it how it was. Now I knew this was absolutely an outrageous decision being I was given thirty to forty minutes to speak and when practiced I spoke for two and a half hours. I know, totally crazy but I just left it.

Normally, when I asked to do special music time during church service I would be so set to go when I asked but come time to sing and I would be a nervous wreck. In fact, I would sit there all through the announcements and collection wishing I had never asked in the first place. I did ask because I felt those times were laid on my heart from God. In the past I hadn't always answered that tug at my heart and wound up feeling horrible because of saying "thanks, but no thanks". One specific time I remember quite clearly was when God laid it on my heart to sing "Silent Night" for my kids. I didn't answer that call until I just couldn't take in anymore. Problem was, it was March and Christmas had long passed. Of course, I had to explain to the congregation why I was singing a Christmas hymn nearly at springtime. I felt like I had to. I know that God had told me a lot sooner to do it but it was that nagging of being disobedient that wouldn't leave me; not until I sang it at least. It came as such a relief to have that nagging feeling gone. Now when I get that tug I do my best to get things done in a timely manner.

It was none other then the hand of God on me the day of the retreat. I arrived and participated in all the events and sat through the first speaker never giving any thought in the least amount that I would soon enough be up on that same platform as the other speakers. Even after all the studying I had done on obedience my mind was absorbing each word spoken and I admired (and was not intimidated by) how each of us were different but how God was using us all the same way that day. Our first session of the day was very rewarding and refreshing. We broke for lunch and then headed back upstairs for part two. I was even able to eat that lunch without any concerns of getting an upset stomach. Again I sat and watched and listened until I was introduced.

There I was. All eyes on me, anticipating what I had to say. It was so incredible how I knew that God was with me in all of this and it gave me a peace and the confidence I needed to get through. I was totally comfortable and just let the words flow out of me. Flow and flow they did. From beginning to end of everything I had written. I'm smiling thinking back on how God worked this all out. Usually, what happens at our retreat is we are always running late but it was different this year. We had a huge gap of over and hour to fill in! Don't worry God had it covered and it was already planted in me that I was going to say what I had to say to get my point across. God knew, and at twenty minutes past the 3pm hour when things should of already been wrapped up I exited the platform and took my seat. Not even a drop of perspiration and that is God at work! With God He can make ALL things possible.

You would think with the retreat behind me now I could move on with a little less of a demand on my time. However, while this was taking place I had also gotten the direction to write the tragedy of Chris down on paper which I had already started working on as well. Along the way, I became aware of a book writing contest that had a deadline of January 31st. Somehow in my own mind I put it together that I was to submit my writings to this contest. I had no idea what this was all about; I just knew that when I was backing away in my thoughts of not doing the writing I couldn't live with that decision. On I typed. There came an even bigger relief when I was able to reach the deadline.

I tried to force the announcement of the winner out of my mind but it would drift there every once in awhile. Wondering if I had won what would God do next. The news did come and I did not win. I was not disappointed; it just kind of filled me with more questions. Questions that I did not have the answer for.

One thought that never left me though was even after I had followed through with entering the book in the contest that I still couldn't get rid of the nagging feeling that I should still be writing a book. What! I thought I had did as asked. Back and forth I went. Yes, I'll do it. No, I already did. Yes, you will. No, I don't want to. I want you to. It's to much for me to handle. Yes, you will. No rest was coming to my mind until finally it was decided. I'll do it in nine months when I am past my official year of mourning. No one can hold back time. There came that knock on my door to my heart once more and this time I knew what had to be done like it or not.

I have come around to liking this project even though for me it is what I consider work. I find it refreshing to be doing something for God. I otherwise, wouldn't be doing this at all if not to serve His purpose. I find it exciting what God may have planned for this book, if anything. I know in human terms what I want this book to accomplish but our plans are not Gods so I look forward to seeing how this plays out.

Honestly, I will be extremely relieved when this work is past.

The "book" was only one of the challenges as this year got under way. Yes, the darts kept flying. Out of my control, was the life choices that others around me made and then the unexpected events.

More poor decisions had been made by our older son. We had thought with two suspensions before the Christmas break that he would make wiser choices. After all, with tears in his eyes, at our meeting with the school that is what he had promised. Now here we were again headed back to the school for a second meeting because that promise had not been fulfilled. This time there would be no more chances and instead he would be expelled. If not for our town offering their services of allowing people to get their diplomas through Adult Education classes then our son would not of received his. With no other alternatives he pulled himself together and got the work completed.

Home life was now more stressful then ever for me. It seemed to me that whenever one of the children were put on restriction they would direct their frustrations at me. Unfair and unrealistic as it was it only created tension. With being expelled from school our older son thought that this meant freedom. Adult Education classes were not on a daily basis and he thought he would have the freedom to do whatever he pleased now that he was "no longer in school". Wrong. His resentment grew to a point that I felt uncomfortable being alone in the same house with him. God is always working and it would turn out that I wouldn't have to spend as many days alone with him as I had figured.

My husband returned home from work one Friday in extreme pain. He had injured his back at work. Now under the circumstances he would have to be out of work until he could recover. He too, would now be home every day. Now our son was going to have to put a cap on his emotions. I have to say, I noticed the change right away. Added to my schedule now was the doctors visits that my husband had to attend. I was happy to do the driving for him; what the downside was is the driving meant we had to travel two and a half hours one way to Portland. It just wasn't a trip to the doctor, it was a day trip and all my responsibilities would have to be rearranged. It wasn't until May that my husband returned to work. For all my husbands suffering I should be thankful though because his pain was an answer to my prayers. I didn't want to be home alone with our older son and God heard my cry. As uncomfortable as my husband was, I was glad to have him home. Count it all joy!

With all the busyness of doctor appointments, typing projects completed, removing Christmas decorations and keeping up with household chores I thought I'd just kind of slide into the coming month of February with a renewed energy. Guess I shouldn't of stretched my neck looking forward and enjoyed the moment because before long I would be right back at square one on emotional breakdown.

My heart was torn open twice more at the arrival of news of two family friends. The first was the news of one of our silver saint ladies in our church family. Her husband had passed away, gone home to be with the Lord. I am sure of that because I just asked him one day if he "had been saved" and he said with a grin that he was. We would be moving soon and I just couldn't go away without knowing if he was saved or not. So there he was picking up his wife from church and I just had to ask before it was to late to get the answer directly from him. I have never regretted that moment.

The second tear to the heart wasn't just a dart it was a bomb shell. We received more tragic news. Our beloved friend, David Reid, had passed away in a skiing accident. Known to many as, "Dr. Dave", as he has a great ministry called Growing Christians Ministries. In fact, we came to know Dr. Dave through his classes that he taught at Groton Bible Chapel in Groton, CT. That is how our friendship with him and his wife grew. They are great people and would do anything for us. That is why when Christopher passed away Dr. Dave offered his services and we did not refuse. Red was grateful to have his support. How were we to know that would be the last visit we would have together. Only God knew we would attend his funeral just four months later. It was like losing another family member. At least I find comfort in knowing without a doubt, that Dr. Dave is enjoying his time up there in heaven. I often wonder if he has seen Chris or not.

It would not be fair at all of me not to mention that you can find Dr. Dave's teachings of the Bible online. You type in www.growingchristan.org

and you'll arrive there to find a treasure of learning. You can pick any book of the Bible of choice and the lessons are done up in fifteen minute segments. Dr.

Dave teaches in a way that gives a clear understanding of the Bible. It gives me great joy to invite you to his website knowing what knowledge you can obtain as I have with his teaching. I hope that you enjoy him as much as we have.

I arrived at the end of January the same as I had entered into it; a heart filled with pain and eyes full of tears.

That was January, eight official months of mourning to go.

February

With saddened hearts we made the trip to CT to attend Dr. Dave's funeral service. I was emotional and did the best I could to get through it all. Red's mom came to the funeral service with us and I found comfort just having her near-by. It was difficult fighting back tears and greet friends of past. Red's back was killing him so we ended up not staying long.

We should try to find the good in things if we can so I set my mind on our visit with Red's mother and sister. Red's sister owns a bakery in New London, CT called, You Take the Cake, so while we were in town we had her whip up a cake for Priscilla. I felt so bad for Priscilla having her birthday fall on the same weekend as the funeral but it couldn't be avoided. We made the best of things and it was nice to celebrate Priscilla turning into a teenager with family.

Sunday morning came soon enough and we sad our good-byes by noon and hit the road once more to head home. It was actually Super Bowl Sunday and we wanted to make it home in time to watch the game. This day was Priscilla's actual birthday and she enjoyed that she would be sharing the day with the big game. Glimmers of joy shining through cracks of pain is what that is.

I too, would disguise my pain as the month continued. I looked forward with eagerness as it approached the times for my favorite Wednesday evening show to begin along with the coming of the Daytona 500. Having others at home and the distraction of the coming events forced me to put away my grief. My time to grieve seemed to keep being stolen from me. Putting others before myself is what God would prefer me to do anyway so I did my best to hold onto that teaching rather then to pout that I couldn't have my "me time".

By the third week of February everyone was home once again as it was winter break. I really didn't have anything planned for fun away from home being our budget was restricted and I think it was somewhat boring for us all. You can only sit around playing board games and watching movies before even that gets old. Red busied himself with work from his job and at times it seemed he wasn't even home. Only our older son seemed to have his presence noted. His past verbal outbursts at me now became silent threatening stares. I however, wasn't silent about anything he directed at me. Most times I would try to ignore his negative behavior toward me and then there were times I just got plain sick and tired of it. When I reached my end in those moments that is when I would burst and out the mouth was the vent. I don't know how many times I have tried to get past this behavior but I did and still do know that it was something I wanted to get past. Yelling does no good for anyone, it only gives you relief in the moment and only leaves hurt built up within each person involved. I have learned along the way, in my Christian walk, how to get beyond this or any other negative behavior. I have found that the more I grow my relationship with Jesus the more that I want to please Him and not to disappoint Him. Like a child that wants to please their parent and not to disappoint them. Well, I didn't want to be a disappointment so more times then not I have learned to bite my tongue. I'm human so I stumble at times and the times I did stumble is when I let bitterness and resentments overtake my thoughts and they would become my leader and not Jesus.

Surprisingly, the one time I decided to keep my mouth shout was the mid-morning that we got the announcement from our older son that he had decided that he was going to run away. This all developed after a heated discussion over powdered milk which ended with him being sent to his room. I used a box of powdered milk to help with the cost of groceries and he had been drinking it all along but on this particular morning he wouldn't have anything to do with it. I also realize, as I'm sure you do, that this was only the straw that broke the camels back. I let Red handle this situation. It would been of no use for me to interfere.

There usually is one member of the family that is considered the rebel and if we were to put a label on our older son he would of taken this title. In fact, that is the title we have given him. Which is kind of humorous considering that he has just recently joined the Army. Anyone that has known him and speaks to us about his career choice all agree that if he is to rid himself of rebellion the Army would be the ones to help him through it. I hope for his sake that he does get through it. Living a life of rebellion is no way to live and such a waste of the precious time that God has granted each of us.

Bradley and Priscilla were now without their second oldest brother. On one hand, I was heartbroken for them knowing that they too were not past the pain of losing Chris. On the other hand, I felt a tremendous relief. I had often prayed for God to get me through the months until their brother turned eighteen so he could join the service and he wouldn't be around any longer to taunt me. Now here he was leaving our home five and a half months sooner then expected. Was that's God's answer? I don't know and still don't know. What I did know was with each passing day it became more apparent to me that he wasn't going to return. I actually began to relax in my home for a change and for that I was happy. I felt like a ton of bricks had been lifted from my back and that is how I moved into the coming month.

That was February, seven official months of mourning to go.

March

With the absence of tension in our home I noticed an air of peace. It felt nice not to think that I had to live constantly looking over my shoulder. I felt a freedom in my own home that I hadn't felt for a long time. It was sad that I had allowed one person to steal my joy and sadder still that I felt enjoyment with that person not directly in my life. Parts of me felt guilty for feeling how I felt but other parts of me felt like I deserved to be happy. After all, look at the battle that I had just come from, don't I deserve a chance to enjoy my life? I put my chin up and decided I was going to enjoy my life regardless of how it came to be.

My main focus now was to help take care of my husband and to help him through with the doctor's orders. My husband's back operation had taken place early in the month and now would be the long drawn out process of healing. I was pleased when he did everything the doctor wanted him to do. This meant extra work for me but was happy to do whatever I had to do knowing that my husband was already having relief in his back.

I was also busy with things that I wanted to do. I had mentioned to my best friend that there would be a craft fair here in town if she wanted to participate in it. She said she would and if I wanted I could put some of my crafts on her table. I didn't have a lot of stuff together so I decided I would make some small leather pouches with some leather scraps I had packed away and I also prepared a batch of goat milk soap and shaped it into eggs. The leather work consumed much of my time so with that and the egg shaped soap I set out to have a day shared with fellowship and not sales. That is exactly what I got too. I didn't sell any of my items but enjoyed watching my friend sell her's. The funny part was her spending her profit at other crafter's tables. We had fun though and our day was topped off with the adventure of having a flat tire await us on our departure.

Life wasn't all fun and games this month as I was still handling the affairs of Christopher. It seemed much to frequent that I would go to the mailbox and find mail concerning him. Mostly it was the mail from the organ donor organization. When we had made the decision to donate Chris's organs we were grateful to be helping others, however, each time I received any mail from the organization it just became a reminder of that painful day that we lost Chris. Receiving mail, even with good intent on their part, only churned my ache in my heart. I missed him and this only reminded me that he wasn't coming back.

Sometimes when I received the mail I wouldn't open it for a few days and other times I would prepare myself with a speech before I opened it. Some of the letters were expressions of thanks and others were to inform us of what was taking place with the organs. I don't think anything could of prepared me for one letter in particular. This letter had actually arrived back in November of 2011.

It was a Saturday morning and I had taken my coffee and devotional along with my Bible and sat in the sun shining through the glass door. After some time with my devotions and prayer I decided to address the mail that was stacked up on the table. One piece of the mail was from the organ donor organization. What now, was my thought as I opened it. I began to read the usual expression of thanks in the first paragraph but this time it ended with a different sentence. This sentence informed me I was going to learn the outcome of our generosity. OUTCOME! This was information that I had been long awaiting. My heart began to race and I started to shake uncontrollably, tears welled up in my eyes and I sobbed loudly as I read the news of the people Chris had given a second chance at life to. I had to tell Red! I found Red and as I approached him he asked me; "What's wrong?" I handed him the letter and stood shaking like a leaf as he read it. In true man fashion, he says, "I don't know what your crying for, this is good news." He wrapped his arms around me until I could calm down. I knew this was good news and am pleased to know that Chris was able to help so many even if it caused me to renew the pain and reality of what it cost to give others what they needed.

The last letter we received about Chris's tissue organs came the third week of March. My reaction to this letter was not as severe as we had been warned in the previous donor letter that we would be receiving a second letter around this time. I was able to read it without the emotional meltdown and pondered about the people Chris would once more be helping. Making a decision for your loved one to be an organ donor is bitter sweet and it is the sweetness that I've planted in my heart.

More bitter sweet was coming my way as spring approached. Spring is my second favorite season and we were headed into it with some unseasonably warm temperatures. The first day of the season would top out at seventy-five degrees followed by temperatures in the eighties the next two days. I enjoyed these days by getting outside and doing a little yard work and going for my morning walks. It was on these walks that my mind would drift to thoughts of Christopher and how once again there was another season that he would not be experiencing. I'd cry the pain away and try not to be to red in the face on my return home. If Red ever noticed my eyes being red he did not say a word.

I moved along enjoying getting ready for the craft fair and soon enough my best friend was spending the night so we could be set up in time for the craft fair the next morning. All was well until we received a phone call. Red had answered the phone because my friend and I were going over some last minute price details for the craft table. Red came out into the dining room to let me know who had called and that is when my world, as I was becoming to know it, came crashing down around me. The phone call came from our rebel runaway asking if he could come visit and discuss moving back home. Instantly, I made a mental scan of my home and what I may have to put away. I hurried up with my task at hand and waited his arrival.

The meeting did not go well. First observance that I made was there wasn't a greeting with a hug to his dad. Not only was our son their but also the gentlemen of the home he was staying with. What it came down to was this man thought it was wrong of him to enable our son in his situation and was no longer going to allow our son to stay in his home. As the conversation continued our son had mentioned a time when he had called our home and I had told him that if he had wanted to speak to his father that I would prefer he called his father at his cell phone. It turned into a you said I said argument and suddenly it was; see I told you how she is. Next thing you know out the door he stomps again. No one followed him until a good ten minutes later and that person was his father. Before he left though I wasn't holding any resentments I was feeling back. I knew it wasn't the right choice but out it all came anyway. During the entire conversation the conclusion was drawn that the only reason our son was in our home wanting to come home was because he had nowhere else to go and this gentlemen he was staying with talked him into coming to see us. I also didn't hold back the resentment I felt having someone come into my home thinking they were going to tell us what they thought was the best way we should handle things with our son. I was not holding back any of my anger. I know this was not what God would of wanted of me and still it took me quite some time to calm down. Only after Red had gone to get our son did I even think to have my friend join us at the dining table. She was in the room but across sitting in the living room space. Later she told me she was praying over there by herself. By the time Red returned home alone I had gotten to a point where I could talk civil. This didn't mean I wanted to continue my conversation and it didn't mean I agreed with everything that was said in the conversation. Yes, I felt foolish for having exploded but isn't there three sides to a story? Your side, my side and then the truth. Well, I knew two of three sides and that gentlemen only had one. So yes, a complete stranger thinks he knows our son and his situation so much better then we do and that put my feathers in a ruffle. I absolutely did not handle this situation beyond my feelings and beat myself up about it until I could see a lesson being taught in it. I definitely didn't welcome our son with open arms because I hadn't reached a point of forgiveness toward him. I would have to reach that point. I put the negative occasion behind me the next day and enjoyed my time at the craft show. I knew I had another spiritual hurdle to get over but for now I just wanted to enjoy my friends company. The peace I entered the month with was certainly not going to be the forefront of my thoughts as I entered yet another new month.

That was March, six official months of mourning to go.

April

Learning the lesson that I should have to find forgiveness toward our son wasn't something that happened over night. After the unpleasant visit we had with him something kept nagging at me. I believe that nagging came from the Holy Spirit. I was unsettled within myself and knew this issue needed to be resolved. I know only one way to have things resolved and that is to go to the Lord in prayer. So I did and these prayers weren't answered right away but they did come sooner then later. I guess my persistence must of paid off. I just wanted to get past these stirred up feelings within me. One day it just became clear to me what I needed to do. Yes, me and not him. Doesn't that just figure? Someone bugs me and I'm the one who has to take the first steps to get past the issue. You'll find that is one way God likes to operate. When we are growing in Gods word it is up to us to take each step closer to Him and lessons that come our way are for us, not always for those around us or the ones directly involved in our circumstance. Acknowledging and doing this alone are steps toward God and letting Him grow you. The feelings that get stirred up within you because of this step you must take forward aren't always pretty either. Just let God know exactly how you are feelings and ask Him to help you get past the turmoil going on inside your mind. You also need to stop replaying the past over and over and focus on your goal of getting past this turmoil. You need to stop the blame game within yourself and choose to do what God would have you do. What is it that God would have us do? To love others as you would love yourself. Make that choice to put the past away and clean that slate off until it is spotless (for that is how God sees us) start over and start fresh and new. This experience will be ever so rewarding when you feel the peace that it brings within you.

Being that the first week of April included the Easter celebration brought forth the reminder of what Jesus did for us on the cross. How could I ignore a lesson of forgiveness when it became so fresh to me once more. Each of us at one time or another may come to a place in life that we need to have forgiveness toward someone. I say go for it! Do it for you and you'll find such a peace from it. A burden lifted and freedom from that past you've let go of. Moving forward in your walk with Jesus and in your life creating something new in that cleaned up space. I find it to be delightful.

Beyond my spiritual growth, life continued on in it's ususal fashion. I took care of as many things as I could for my husband as he continued to heal, ran the household and tried to keep the finances afloat. That is why when my husband expressed to me that he wanted to take another trip to CT at the end of the month to attend the Spring Sizzler at Stafford Motor Speedway I nearly fainted. You've got to be kidding? How was this extra expense going to make me feel secure in my world. With the lack of funds we were already facing how was this to be a wise financial decision? I didn't bother to express all of what I felt and I let it go and he had his way. After all, he reminded me how for the last five years he had given up this event. He also reminded me that God has always provided all that we've ever needed. I couldn't argue with that.

We stayed at Red's mom house during our time in CT. This gave Red the chance to do some chores for his mom that she had asked him to take care of. I left them to themselves and decided to go visit my brother, or brothers as it turned out. That is why I'm thankful for the state of mind I was in. I was very much at peace within myself and seemed like I was just floating along through the day. I was letting others act and letting myself react instead of taking the lead. I believe that is the only way I was able to make it through the visit with the younger of my two brothers. I hadn't seen or spoken with my youngest brother in over five years. This was due to a disagreement between my husband and my brother and that business is their's.

However, my brother choose to make me part of their affairs by withholding me from his life. He did, however, take my unexpected visit as an opportunity to vent his years of bottled up frustrations out on me. After doing so I asked what I ever did to him and his only reply was because I'm with my husband. So, guilty by association. I didn't allow his distaste for my presence hinder my visit with my older brother and his daughter. I hadn't expected to see my younger brother so his presence was just an added bonus for me. I wasn't going to let something I had nothing to do with that happened over five years ago rule my time now. Be it that my younger brother did is sad but it was comical. What a true example of not letting go of the past.

Our visit with Red's mom ended Sunday morning as she headed off to church and we headed for Stafford. The morning was so bright and beautiful with the warmth of the sunshine and the singing of birds. It was a prefect day for the opening of the racetrack.

The familiar view of the parking lot and stands made us feel like we were home again. After getting our tickets we let the children loose, as we always had, to visit their favorite race cars and drivers. Red and I made it through the packed crowd to visit some old friends as well. It was nice to see some familiar faces in such a large crowd. It had been a long time since I have been around such a large crowd and as memories of the past began to stir in my heart and mind I was relieved when they announced that the races were about to begin and everyone was to find a seat. My memories were hard to keep at bay with as many times as we had visited this race track. It became a ritual every Friday evening after Red got out of work that we would head up to the races in Stafford. We'd pack the car and all six of us would head up to enjoy a race car packed night. Now we were four. Memories came flooding forth of all that we had been through since our last visit here. I couldn't help but think of how much the children had grown and how different our world was now. Not only from the lack of having two of our children with us but to realize how far we had come in our spiritual walk with Jesus. It was almost as if we had taken a trip back in time watching as we saw familiar people doing their usual routine. I felt like a stranger amongst all this familiarity.

I got my head back in the game by paying attention to the excitement the children were having. It was amazing to me how many names and race car numbers they each remembered. We stayed right up until the final lap. I couldn't believe how quickly it all seemed to pass. Before I knew it we were once again on the road headed back to our home in Maine. I was amazed that such a simple trip home turned into something so spiritually rewarding and thanked God for pulling me even closer to Him.

That was April, five official months of mourning to go.

May

With spring upon us the warming temperatures brought forth a renewed eagerness to prepare for the summer months. After all the cold of winter and seemingly short summers here in Maine I look forward to feeling the sun upon my skin as much as possible. Once more I would force the issue by setting up my patio furniture to soon. It would be all set up looking so inviting then it would seem as if the spring rains would never end. The rains did end though come mid May with the high temperatures reaching the lower eighties it made for a comfortable morning sipping my coffee outside. As long as the bugs stayed at bay that would be were I'd get my start to the day with my morning devotions and prayer time.

With May also came the final days of Red's healing process. After five months he would be getting back to work and of all days, it was his birthday. Returning to work would improve our financial state so to me it was a great birthday gift.

It seemed forever since I was able to have some alone time and was grateful I'd have some time to myself before the children's release from school for their summer vacation. I took care of more chores but also found enjoyment getting my seeds prepared for my garden. I even made myself another batch of goat milk soap. I also started taking walks more often because my husband said it looked like the dog was getting fat. The dog?

We did make one big change in our lives during April that we continued on with into May and will last until God says to do something different. That change was attending a different church. The church we were attending and was so adamant that God had placed us in finally had hired a new pastor. We were going to find a church closer to our community about nine months earlier but that is when the pastor moved and there was the need to have someone fill in. With the pulpit now filled we made our move to a church closer to home. A lovely decision it has been.

We visited once in April then missed the week we went to CT but now we attend regularly. We have felt right at home from the very first visit. Everyone there is quite friendly and makes us feel very welcome. We unknowingly met the Pastor for the first time when he welcomed us the first morning we attended. Later when we listened to the sermon we realized whom he was. We spoke with him again before we departed. I don't recall exactly what we all talked about but one thing I do remember is when this gentleman spoke to us he looked us in the eye. That alone spoke volumes to me. That to me meant sincerity. We've also come to learn that he has a great sense of humor. Best of all he teaches directly from the Bible and God has given him the gift of being a great speaker. Once again, God has placed us right where we needed to be.

During these first few weeks and on into June our pastor had been teaching us to wrap our minds around living in the "now". Not dwelling on the past and not to worry about what tomorrow may bring.

It's not like I haven't heard all this before but I was hearing it again in a new light. I wanted to be here and I wanted to be in the "now" but parts of me weren't cooperating. I still was having difficulty at times fighting off the feelings of depression trying to pull me down. Overall, I seemed like I was a normal person but when I was alone my thoughts would often drift toward Christopher. This is fine, but what would happen is the thoughts were always replaying what went on at the hospital that dreaded October weekend. I could of very easily let myself slip into that negative thought pattern and it was only with Gods grace that He placed us in a new church when He did.

I would find myself in thought and next thing you know I would be thinking about Christopher. It could be anything so simple as a sunny day I thought he was missing that would start the wheels spinning in my head. Then there once again I would be, standing in the hospital room holding his hand once more. I knew this wasn't right thinking and knew it could become unhealthy. I was aware of my behavior and therefore knew I had already taken the first step of acknowledgment. I would have the awareness of where my thoughts were leading me and I would at that point literally talk out loud to myself. I would say things like. "Okay, just stay right here." "You know Chris is being taken care of in heaven so don't cry." "I'm right here, I'm right here and it is a beautiful day." "Enjoy this day, this day." "This day is now." It was those minds sets that would pull me back into the moment and the more I have stayed in the moment the less my mind drifts. God has used my pastor to give me my life back and for that I am thankful beyond what words can express. To God be the glory! He always knows what we need when we need it.

That was May, four official months of mourning to go.

June, July, August

I don't want to disappoint anyone by putting June, July and August together in one chapter but this time here is all about summer vacation. Also, remember that I am still experiencing time feeling as one long day.

I knew the children would be out of school soon but when that day arrived I felt so unprepared for it. In years past I normally would have things laid out for us to do and keep the children as busy as possible. This was my way of trying to keep them out of trouble. With this coming vacation it took me a few days to get my mind wrapped around that summer vacation was even upon us and that I better start getting some events planned.

With the warmer months comes the chores of yard clean-up so that is where I decided to start. I try to teach the children responsibilities first and fun second. First order of business was our goat barn. That chore we all tackled and was able to complete in one day. Thank goodness we only have one stall to clean. Priscilla and I would take turns filling the wheelbarrow and then Bradley would empty the contents in the compost pile that I was trying to get started. It was hot and dusty and we were all glad when it was over. Our only other huge chore that we have for taking care of the goats is getting the loft full of hay for the coming winter. That we also did in one day and that wasn't all that fun either. The three of us put up one hundred bales in one day and we were very happy to have that taken care of. I tried to look on the positive side and told them at least we had only used two days of our summer to get the goat chores taken care of. If only our firewood chore could be minimized into that amount of time.

Now, I tell you, God works in your life even when we aren't aware of it. This subject of firewood is a good time to tell you of a struggle that was running through my mind. This struggle was of having a constant reminder of Chris. It's not like I don't want to think about Chris; it's just that some things remind me of what Chris is no longer doing or will have or what may have been. Getting my firewood brought upon me these thoughts. At the time of Chris's accident he had been working about five miles from here in a local garage; the same company that I order my firewood from. Well, this year to avoid any reminders of this hurt within me I had wanted to find a different place to order my firewood. As God would have it, He didn't want me sidestepping anything. Let's just face this discomfort head on, shall we?

I did everything humanly possible to find a new place to order my firewood. I had gotten a list of three new places that I could call and went about trying to get a hold of someone to place my order. Needless to say, I wasn't getting any responses. I was beginning to wonder if I would find anyone to fill my order and be able to get my firewood started on time. I would, but I didn't know it at the time but God did.

In the meantime, Priscilla had gotten an invitation to visit some of her neighboring friends. I was making my way down the dirt road to her friends house when we came upon a pick-up truck and some type of brush-hog cutting machine both blocking the roadway. I sat there for more time then I would of wanted to wondering if anyone even saw me waiting to drive through. Instead of continuing to sit and wonder I decided to get out of the car and let them know I was there. Wouldn't you know it! The man I acknowledged was one of the owners of the logging company I get my firewood from! I'd be a fool not to realize that this wasn't any random appointment. We needed firewood and I wasn't going to miss out on this opportunity to ensure that we would have it. I sucked it up and took care of business and told myself I would just have to get through the emotions of it all when that time came. At the moment I was just glad to know my order was in and it was only a matter of time before we'd have to start that chore.

I ordered our firewood at the beginning of July and thought we probably wouldn't see it until September.

As it turned out, with having less of a "mud season" I was pleasantly surprised when our delivery came at the beginning of August. I was so excited when we got it, I couldn't wait to start cutting and splitting it. I'd have to wait though because I didn't have my new chain for the saw and I hadn't gotten what gas and oil I would need. Yet again, I wasn't prepared like I had been in the past but I told myself it didn't matter anyway because I wouldn't be able to get started cutting because we were headed out of town that coming weekend.

Back in January I had made a promise to Red's mom and I wasn't about to break it. She had been held up for quite some time with back problems and wasn't able to keep her house up to her usual standards so I told her that I would come down over the summer and help her get things back in order. We made the trip down to CT once again and I along with the children fulfilled that promise. We spent every waking minute possible "spring cleaning" her home with mom helping and one day with her daughters help. Each night we were rewarded with a night out for dinner. That promise complete I had also told the children I would take them camping.

My sister and her boyfriend have had a campsite for a number of years and they were spending their summer there once again this year. It gave me the opportunity to give the children a camping experience and a chance to have a visit with my sister. Both of which were accomplished as I set my sites on returning home once more.

During the last few weeks that the children were still in school I thought that I had come up with a brilliant idea. We have had dirt bikes for quite some time but never seem to be able to ride them as much as we would like. My plan was to get the children back into this hobby by making a dirt bike track. Up on the back side of our property would be the best location for the children to ride their dirt bikes. For the past two summers I had been back there with the children and many times by myself already clearing out sticks and branches that had been left behind when the lot had been cleared of its pine trees. I continued to do more clearing with the children concentrating only on the path that we were going to build our track. I had already started the clearing when they were attending school so when vacation started and they had seen the progress I had made it filled them with excitement to keep the project going. I thought I was killing three birds with one stone with this project! The portion of the track that I had been working on was filled with wild red raspberry bushes. I'm sure you know how many thorns can be on a raspberry bush! I would take up the wheel barrel and fill it as much as possible and then feed the plants to the goats. The goats love them and never seem to mind the thorns. I was clearing out my lot, building a track for the children and getting food for my goats! Eventually, our track was complete and the children were back to a much loved hobby. It felt great that we had accomplished what we had set out to do. I was proud of them for sticking with it. This task wasn't a one day event; it had taken us up into the middle of August before it was complete. The children didn't mind though because we knew we wouldn't have to stop riding until the first snowfall. Our plans were to have as much fun on our new track as possible.

Our summer wasn't all work and no play. We had our fair share of fun. The summer became filled with swimming, tubbing, fishing, bicycle riding, racing, summer camp for Priscilla, sleep overs, trips to the movie theater, picnics and finally school clothes shopping. Before I knew it the children had to get back to school at the end of August. For a summer I didn't plan we sure had a ton of fun which for a pleasant change outweighed the chores.

We did attend two events during summer vacation that I want to tell you about with more details. One was our older son graduating from his adult education program. This I want to mention because going to this event wasn't as simple as a decision as you may think. After all that my husband and I had gone through with our sons education it left a spot hardened in my heart. I was still working on my forgiveness lesson which meant I still was harboring resentment in my heart. Back and forth with this decision of attending or not became a battle within me. I knew the right thing to do but I didn't want any part of a celebration. This came as no celebration to me at all. It was more like a huge pile of bricks being taken off my back. After all the battles that took place with homework, teachers, detentions, suspensions, being passed through the system; I was just sick of all of it. Then to hear people give him praise for sticking with his education after becoming expelled; I'm sorry but that really got under my skin! Hence, the battle that went on inside me was none to pleasant. I knew this wasn't right thinking and I set out to fix this wrong thinking. I prayed often and then went into studying about forgiveness which lead into studies on loving one another, which lead into being obedient to the truth through the Spirit. That spirit being the Holy Spirit. That is why I was having such a battle within myself. I, me, my mind, my heart was in war with what the Holy Spirit would want me to do. So during my studying I came across a passage that helped me get past my thinking and into Gods thinking. That passage I found in the Bible reminded me that those who walk with Jesus do so with love for one another, even to love fervently if necessary; it also says to do it with a pure heart. Over the coming days before this graduation took place I came to the point where I was able to do this. I had a choice to make and if I was to walk with Jesus I knew the right choice was to put away the anger of the past and be grateful for all the positive that was taking place for our older son. I attended the graduation and actually enjoyed myself. I was thankful for the peace I felt in my heart.

Another event that took place during this summer was on July 15th. I point out the exact date because this was a very special day for me and heaven. I was baptized! Of all the lakes around I was able to be baptized right here in our own Sebec Lake. That is the very first lake that I ever visited when I came to Maine and the lake that we do all our summer events in being we live just up the road from the local boat launch. That is not all that made the day special for me.

Before the baptismal took place, Red, my best friend and I were sitting in our lawn chairs chatting. We had a great view of the lake and the clear blue sky above. While we were talking I was looking around and that is when I spotted something in the sky. Upon closer observation we all concluded that what we saw soaring around back in forth in the sky was a bald eagle! I hadn't seen an eagle since that time I was outside laying in the grass crying that sunny afternoon. I knew this was Chris's favorite bird and I couldn't help but think that seeing this bird was his way of telling me that he was with us that day. I may sound like a fruit loop to you but my heart was telling me something different.

I was experiencing something else over the summer that I found quite interesting at first which turned into curiosity then just outright frustrating to me. As I would have my devotion and prayer time each morning I would take time and enjoy the view out of our glass doors. I noticed a puddle in our driveway that Bradley and I had filled with crushed stone but not enough to solve the puddle issue. I realized that the water had made a heart shaped puddle. I smiled as I thought about all the rocks we had collected over the years shaped like hearts. Then I started to notice heart shapes everywhere I went. Stones pressed in the pavement, clouds, stains on my clothes, water droplets, dirt marks, even a tiny crumb I'd picked up. What was going on! I got to the point I would point them out to whomever was around because it just was getting crazy. At first I thought maybe that was Chris's way of letting me know he was around then I got thinking maybe someone was trying to tell me I had some sort of heart disease then I thought maybe Satan was trying to mess with my mind. It just got out of hand. It was so out of hand that at one point I thought of naming this chapter: My Heart Shaped Summer. Instead, what I did was pray to God. I just told Him that whatever the reason that this was happening that I just didn't understand and could He please put an end to it. I noticed that it all stopped and even when I tried to find something heart shaped I couldn't.

Two other matters came up over the summer that concerned the heart as well, but this wasn't a heart shape it was a heart matter. We had told our son that when he was eighteen that we would give him all the belongings he left in our home. I don't like broken promises so on his birthday I brought all his possessions to him. I thought we had a good visit. He showed me around the farm he was working at and then a few things he had purchased over the past months and we even sat down and had a long talk. We both cried and discussed some past issues and that is when I suggested that we all just need to clean the slate. The past was behind us and he had good things to look forward to and lets just start fresh. I left believing that we would only grow forward in our relationship.

The second matter of the heart had happened the first week of June. I had gotten a phone call back in April from the organ donor bank and they had asked me if we minded receiving mail from one of Chris's organ recipients. I had told the woman we wouldn't mind at all and she told me to expect something in the mail form the organ bank. I was nervous but also excited to hear from someone. Even when the envelope arrived it still flooded me with emotion. The thank you card expressed the gratitude of the recipient and the second chance at life that they were given. Red and I are very happy for them. We lost Chris in our lives, but they have a life to live now with their family that they never thought they would have. It is amazing to me still how I can't seem to wrap my mind around what it must feel like to receive that gift. On our side of the matter, we are pleased that God was able to use Chris in the life of someone else yet again. This ripple continues, amazingly so.

Receiving this card only brought tears to my eyes once. I read the card over and over until one of those times I noticed when the card was dated. It tore at my heart strings but I looked at it as another gift. The card was dated on my husbands birthday.

So with more highs then lows I was able to make it through my summer. I wasn't looking forward to the children going back to school being we were having so much fun. All good things come to an end, so it was back to the grindstone when school started. It was only the chill that started to fill the air that forced me into the fact that summer was coming to an end.

That was my June, July, August one official month of mourning to go.

September

September is Christopher's birth month. I knew this day was approaching, what I didn't know is how much it was bothering me. Christopher had his accident on the first day of October and died on the third so throughout the past year I couldn't help but remember counting each month as they passed. It wasn't even until the end of September that I was aware of how I had been effected by his approaching birth date. I noticed I had the feeling that a cloud had lifted from me. A cloud that I wasn't even aware was covering me. I thought all this time that I was being strong and passing through these "anniversary" moments unscaved. With the arrival of this renewed feeling I took the time to review what I thought to be normal weeks for me. I didn't like the review though. I noted how tired I seemed to be all to often, how unsocial I had become at church and I was short tempered toward the children. I was glad that this time was passing.

After much thought, I put a finger on what was bothering me. All this time when I thought of Chris I was able to think of him as still being part of our lives. Now with the passing of his birthday I would no longer be able to use the phase "remember last year when Chris….". All the "last year" memories wouldn't include Chris. It felt like for the first time I would actually be moving on without him. No longer would he be in my life but the life we shared would only be memories. I didn't want memories, I wanted Chris back. I wanted him to see me in my new glasses, I wanted him to see our new car and the new boat we bought. I wanted him to see my stonewall I was building, I wanted him to know our cat had run away and that this year we still planned on going to the Fryeburg Fair. I just wanted him to be around. It still feels like we have a piece of the puzzle missing. I would be ending my "official mourning" period this month but that wouldn't mean my hurt was gone.

Knowing that Chris's birth date was approaching come September, I had begun to pray about it in August. My heart ached that we wouldn't be able to watch Chris grow up into his life as a young man. God knew I was hurting this way but I told Him anyway. I also prayed to God that He would give me some kind of a distraction to get me through the actual day. I guess this was one of those moments when we should be careful of what we ask for.

We started our September Sunday morning like any other and continued with our afternoon routine as well. That went for me and Red anyway. It was a sunny day and after a few days of rain the children wanted to get outside. We didn't have a problem with that; so off they went to enjoy their dirt bikes. Just a normal day suddenly turned "da ja vo".

I watched my son laying on the hospital cart as we waited for the doctor to return with some sort of news on his condition. My son was trying to be brave but I could see concern all over his face. Upon the doctors return, he thanked us for coming in. I instantly knew something was wrong. "Due to your sons injuries we are going to have to send him to Bangor". Flashes of bright lights and tubes and blood flew through my mind. I told myself to remain focused on what the doctor was telling me. I had heard that statement before. "We are going to transport him by ambulance." The all to familiar waiting game began as we were left alone waiting on the arrival of the EMT's.

Weather they arrived in a timely manner or I'm just used to waiting I'm not sure of but the EMT's came and rolled Bradley away. As they prepared him for his trip to Bangor the female EMT made a comment to Bradley that stopped me in my tracks. I detected by what she had said that she very well could of been the same EMT that arrived at the scene of Chris's accident. In that moment I was sure of it! Was this the same women that gave Chris the shot to sedate him to prevent further injury to himself? The shot that put Chris to sleep? The shot that prevented me from being able to talk to Chris in the emergency room? The shot that may have prevented Chris from telling them where he hurt. The shot that may have prevented Chris from telling them he was having trouble breathing? The shot is a routine method to prevent further injury and that's all it was and she was only doing her job. I have obviously struggled with that shot but with time and prayer have settled on knowing God used it as part of His plan.

I called Red and informed him of the news on Bradley. We met each other at the local garage and made our way to Eastern Maine Medical Hospital. The evening once more brought flashes of the past in my mind.

Red had called a neighbor and asked if Priscilla could spend the night so she could attend school the next morning as we would be having a long night in the hospital. We could now give our full attention to the matter at hand. Our ride to the hospital was almost a carbon copy of the night we drove to Bangor to be with Chris. The wind was causing the leaves to fly around and once more it was rainy. With the exception of the excitement of almost hitting a bull moose our ride remained quiet.

We parked our car in our "usual" section of the parking lot and made our way to the emergency room where we were told to meet up with Bradley. Each step I took became heavier as memories flooded my mind of being in these same hallways less then a year ago. I reminded myself to stay focused on Bradley as we completed our journey to the emergency room.

Just like with Chris, we didn't have to wait in the outside waiting area with everyone else. Red let the nurse at the desk know who we were and they lead us directly to Bradley. We all sat and talked as we waited on the results of Bradley's injury. An injury he received from his dirt bike hand grip when it was rammed up under his right rib cage.

While Red and I were on the coach enjoying a football game the children were out enjoying riding their dirt bikes. Their enjoyment came to an abrupt end when Priscilla rounded the fourth turn and discovered Bradley on the ground. He had come around the turn to quickly and wasn't able to prevent his dirt bike from running into a stump. His front tire partially collied with the tree stump and made his front forks twist abruptly to the left. On impact, this threw Bradley forward landing on his left hand grip directly under his right rib cage. In the world of racing dirt bikes this is called cross-up. The doctor eventually arrived to tell us that this cross-up left Bradley with a four inch laceration to his liver. No wonder the doctor back in Dover-Foxcroft thanked us for coming in. What he didn't tell us then was that if Bradley had ripped his liver another inch he would of damaged it beyond repair. I don't even want to give that any thought. What I did do instead was thank God that Bradley in due time was going to be healed. With four and one half days in the hospital and a few reminders to slow down he did just that. Before I knew it, he was headed back to school.

This event all began on Sunday, September 10, 2012. A Sunday that would of been Chris's nineteenth birthday. I had prayed for a distraction to help me get through that day and that is exactly what I was given. A distraction that I could of lived without in many ways. Next time I think to pray for a distraction maybe I should weigh that up against what it would be if I just walked through my circumstance. After all, I never gave any thought to all Chris's future birth dates that would occur; only the first. Maybe I was meant to face it.

As September neared its end I set my sights on the coming weeks. I was nearing the end of my official year of mourning. The events that we work our way through that society allows us to have as healing time. A time were we have gone through all our first's. A time that society excuses our behaviors knowing we have lost someone dear to us. A time that "officially" ends when it is marked by the first anniversary. There is nothing "official" about mourning. There are choices of what to do in that mourning though. As our first year anniversary of Chris's passing approached we decided we would do what we would of normally done. That normal for us was attending Woodsman Day at the Fryeburg Fair. Chris would of wanted us to.

That was September 2012, three days of official mourning to go.

October

It's amazing to me what one can do when they set their mind to it. The entire year that I had faced ahead of me was all about choice and I was amazing myself. I had made the choice to live and keep moving forward with my life and to grow from my lose of Chris. This is not to say it was easy but with God in my life it was possible. I have been challenged to rise above my emotions and when I faltered I choose to get up brush off and keep taking more steps. That is why at the home stretch of the arrival of Chris's anniversary of his passing that you wouldn't of found me at home crying my eyes out. The cloud that followed me around from Chris's birthday didn't stop me from doing other things in my life. Being we had made plans to go the Fryeburg Fair I had been doing some work around town to earn some extra cash. I spent hours painting a near-by camp and enjoyed knowing

I would be able to spend my money freely. Six days of work and one day of fun. It all seemed worth it to me. After all, God took six days to create the universe we live in and rested on the seventh day; guess I couldn't ask for any better example then that.

There wasn't any quilt or shame attending the fair ither. If Chris was here on earth we probably would of called him to see if he wanted to go with us. Once again, he was out on his own and by his schedule he would of had to of been at his job. Whether he could of taken the day off remains unseen and remember he probably wouldn't of thought it "cool" to go with his parents. Probably, probably, probably. If, if, if. They weren't choices I could make. I choose to enjoy my day with my husband and the other two children we did have with us and create new memories. I found it rewarding and it put joy in my heart. I call this choice, "productive living".

Shortly around the bend of Chris's passing anniversary came the anniversary of his memorial service. Another day that isn't a pleasant memory and one I don't allow my mind to dwell upon for to long. This year that date landed exactly on Christopher Columbus Day. Go figure! The day we all celebrate together as a family by getting out and taking a hike atop a mountain would now be shadowed by a past tragedy. As God would have it though, the day wouldn't be of doom and gloom; it became a day of freedom.

The previous Sunday we attended our Sunday Bible Study and Worship Service. After our Bible Study I told Red that I wasn't going to attend the Worship Service because I wasn't feeling well. I went out to our Suburban and tried to make myself comfortable for the next hour. I didn't want to be out in the parking lot and was beating myself up about it. That is when I turned my thoughts toward God. I figured I could still pray while I was out there, so that is what I did. Afterward, I was just laying there with my head rested against the door. I was just kind of resting with no real focus on any thoughts when suddenly and ever so gently a thought that was not my own crossed my mind. It was like a breath of air crossing over my forehead from right to left. It was a thought that made me sit up straight. This thought spoken to me was this: Take Chris's ashes on Columbus Day and spread them on the mountain. I wasn't even thinking about Chris in that moment and bam; there the thought was. Now my thoughts were of how I was going to get Red to agree with this "thought".

Like with any relationship, bringing certain subjects up sometimes requires timing. That is what I thought I would need when approaching this subject of Chris's ashes with Red. I didn't want to mention it to him when the children where around so I waited until he had called me from work. I told him of my experience in the Suburban and also added that I think we should do it, being this would be the last year that all the family could attend. Soon enough, our oldest would be off to the Army and being that I was told to do it I thought that would mean the coming Columbus Day not any other. After a few days of thought, Red agreed. He also agreed he should be the one to call Chris's brother.

Red had arranged it that we would be picking up Chris's brother in downtown Dover-Foxcroft then from there head out for our hike. We had arrived a little later then previous years because once again as I had done ten years earlier on Columbus Day, I locked the keys in the car.

Thank God that Red wasn't able to throw a fit. Just minutes after our discovery of this unfortunate mishap, a gentlemen from our church walked by. We informed him of our dilemma and without hesitation he offered to bring Red home a half hours drive away. God's timing is great! That is also why we never minded being late because as we were headed up the mountain everyone there that had arrived earlier were now headed down the mountain. With the exception of a handful of other people, we had the mountain pretty much to ourselves. That made it possible to spread Chris's ashes without interruption. Can you see as clearly as I can, God at work here? His timing is everything.

With the spreading of Christopher's ashes came the feeling of a chapter closing. When we had the memorial service for Chris a few of our friends had asked us if we would be having a grave side service as well. No, was our answer to that and when they asked what we were going to with the urn I just told them that we would keep it with us. Our thoughts then was that when Red passed away that Chris's ashes would be buried next to his. Red and I had talked about where we would spread Chris's ashes if we were going to do it and never was able to figure out what spot would make sense. When I was given the thought to spread them on the mountain it just all came together with the day and date and location. God's timing yet again.

We had kept Chris's ashes in our bedroom next to his cross and ballcap. I had grown emotionally tired of having to see the urn time after time. I kept reminding myself that Chris was in heaven but it still wore me down. The spreading of his ashes gave me freedom to have a peace within me and it was another burden of a constant reminder lifted from me. As we left the mountaintop, I couldn't help this feeling that we were leaving Chris behind. Over and over I repeated that Chris is in heaven and that is only his body. I continued repeating this to myself until any feelings of leaving him behind left my thoughts. We must remember to keep our mind focused upon God, otherwise, we become an easy target for Satan. That cat is always lurking around waiting to pounce. Don't give him the opportunity.

Our Columbus Day of 2012 completed our official time of mourning. When this time arrived it didn't seem possible the last year had passed so quickly. Now we would be headed into the ranks of someone who lost there loved one over a year ago so now I guess it's not supposed to hurt so much. My reality is, my heart still aches on how much I miss Chris. I think of him often and would love for him to have shared in more of our lives. I miss him and want him back but that is NOT how it's going to be. I've accepted this and now allow God to grow me from this pain. I still ache inside, it's just not at the forefront of my thinking. What is at the forefront of my mind is how can I use this circumstance for the glory of God.

MISS YOU

I watch the sky and I wonder
I bow my head and pray
Your with our Lord now
What is it you do from day to day?

Your "time" is not the same
Your world is light and full of love
My world remains the same
Yet different as my time passes by

Deep inside my heart aches
I live daily pushing down this pain

Do you hear me when I talk to you?
Do you hear me sing my songs for you?
Do you hear me when I call your name?
Knowing right well you won't be answering.

I know I'll be with you again
In God's heaven; without end
Each day moves me closer to where you are
When I remember this you don't seem so far

For now I have this moment
Though you are not here
I hold in my heart our memories
That makes life easier to bear

November 2011   By: amber b.

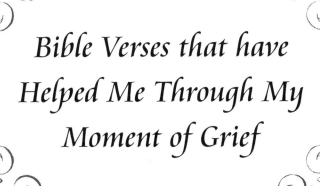

Bible Verses that have
Helped Me Through My
Moment of Grief

I saiah 55:8 "For My thoughts are not your thoughts, Nor are your ways My ways", says the Lord

This verse helped me most to stay in the present moment. It helped me to put away my tears. God sees the bigger picture of taking Chris home as I do not. I would repeat to myself over and over God did not do this to hurt me; He loves me.

Mark 8:35 For whoever desires to save his life will lose it, but whoever loses his life for My sake and the gospel's will save it.

This verse reminds me I live my life to serve Jesus and to put Him first, always. When I do things in my life they are to have the purpose of glorifying Jesus. I will deny the sinful self-serving ways of this world and gain eternity in God's kingdom by excepting Jesus as my Lord and Savior and living by the standards He has set.

Matthew 19:21 Jesus said to him, "If you want to be perfect, go, sell what you have and give to the poor, and you will have treasure in heaven; and come, follow Me.

Since Chris has left us I've learned that I don't need to chase after material possessions. What I need to do is know who Jesus is and be a living example of Him. God will perfect me along the way but what I do know I am to share with others so that they too may decide to follow Jesus. Is it better that I give you a gift that will in time waste away or give you the gift that is offered to all and lasts forever? That gift is from Jesus and it is eternal life in God's kingdom. (see John 3:16)

Matthew 5:4 Blessed are those who mourn, For they shall be comforted.

I know I'm not alone in my trials when I read this verse. When I hurt it is for a purpose. Trying to stay focused beyond my pain is what pulls me through my pain.

Luke 22:26 But not so among you; on the contrary, he who is greatest among you, let him be as the younger and he who governs as he who serves.

Remain humble, is what speaks to me when reading this verse. I am a servant of the Lord and I do all things for Him, not for self gain. We should never think of ourselves above any position that God puts us in.

Luke 5:11 So when they had brought their boats to land, they forsook all and followed Him.

This is a great verse to meditate upon while doing some self examining. What are we willing (or not) to give up for Jesus? Your answers to this question may come to you differently when all seems right with your life opposed to when circumstances take a turn for the worse. I suggest posting this question in a spot where you will see it on a regular basis. That way you may compare your answers when times are smooth to when things aren't going as you may want them to be. Even journal your answers comparing where your heart is and ask yourself why you may have the thoughts you're having. Revealing your thoughts honestly will help you to become aware of where you are at and how would Jesus want you to handle the circumstance. Personally, I find this practice very rewarding.

Psalm 116:15 Precious in the sight of the Lord is the death of His saints.

There was a celebration when Chris was welcomed into Gods kingdom. Chris was home, surrounded with love. What more could I have asked for?

Psalm 147:3 He heals the broken hearted And binds up their wounds.

I am not alone in my sorrow; God watches over me. In time my heart will mend.

Philippians 4:13 I can do all things through Christ who strengthens me.

Removing doubt gives me the ability to keep moving forward. With Jesus always with me and His word planted in my heart I can walk with confidence.

Hebrews 13:8 Jesus Christ is the same yesterday, today and forever.

Jesus is someone I can count on. This verse lifts my spirit knowing I can trust His word and puts a smile on my face.

John 18:11 So Jesus said to Peter, "Put your sword into the sheath. Shall I not drink the cup which my Father has given Me."

Not all things in our lives are going to be comfortable. Keep in your mind and heart that all things are for the purpose of serving Gods plan. Good, bad or indifferent we are to complete His will. Keep your mind focused on His will and not on how you are going to be effected.

Psalm 90:12 Teach us to number our days, that we may gain a heart of wisdom.

I no longer take my life for granted, living as if tomorrow is promised to me. I thank God each day I wake up and try to make my days fulfilling.

God is Ever Present

D o you remember how I told you how God used my daily devotionals to get my attention? Well, during my search to share Bible verses with you I decided to go back to that day that God asked me "Are You Ready?". In my search I discovered God wasn't only reaching out to me on that one day. His attempt to speak to me continued all eleven days before Chris had his accident. However, my mind was distracted by the old wives tale that I didn't see what was right in front of me. The following is a list of verses to go along with each daily devotional study. It amazes me what I have discovered and have decided to make these verses into a study with the purpose of examining myself.

God was with me all along in those eleven days. I just never put the puzzle together until now. Maybe these were just back-up verses if He didn't get my attention right away. It was three days before I promised Him whatever would come that I would be ready, even without being aware that these verses were right in front of me. I don't know if I would of been any different during that tragic time or not. I only know what was and that was Him getting my attention and me making a promise never grasping that He continued to use my daily devotional to speak with me.

Day 1: 2 Peter 3:9 The Lord is not
slack concerning His promise.

The lesson of this daily devotion was that Jesus promised to return to earth again one day. However, with the lesson being titled the same exact title as another devotional that I study (Are You Ready?) was what sparked something within me that I knew God was speaking to me.

These titles were the attention getters followed up with me finding an old scrap of paper and then finally the commercial. Gods knows every bit of us and He knew how to get my attention; and that He did.

Day 2: Matthew 5:4 Blessed are those who
mourn, for they shall be comforted.

This lesson was teaching that it is okay to cry and that when our heart aches so does Jesus's. We are also reminded once again that someday there will be no more tears and that pains of this world will become a thing of the past. (Revelation 21:4) Even Jesus's heart hurts for us when we hurt and He knows that the bigger picture has no pain! Right now though, in the rawness of your circumstance, it's okay to cry. If your not turning to God in prayer for comfort then it is very possible that God will send someone into your life that will help you through this difficult time. It's also possible that God could be using this circumstance to grow you closer to Him and for those of you who don't have Him in your life then this could be Him calling to you to reach out to Him now. My answer to finding comfort has been to cry when I have the need and turn to God in prayer before, during and after my tears. I feel stronger and prepared to keep moving forward when I lay all my circumstances at Jesus's feet.

Day 3: John 5:40 But you are not willing
to come to Me that you may have life.

What I took away from this devotional lesson was that we eventually come to a point in our lives that we will question the subject of God. God will not force Himself into our heart, we must invite Him in. We must be willing and when we do we become part of His family. Gods family will live forever in His kingdom.

Day 4: Psalm 96:10 The Lord reigns; the world also is firmly established, it shall not be moved; He shall judge the peoples righteously.

This daily devotional lesson was teaching us that only Gods judgement is flawless. Life at times doesn't seem fair and that is how I felt when Chris was laying in his hospital bed. I didn't want God to take Chris so early in his life but that was what was happening. God is in control of all things and He has a plan and nothing is going to change that plan. In the end we will all stand before Him and I am thankful that He is a God of love.

Day 5: Exodus 6:6 I am the Lord; I will bring you out from under the burdens of the Egyptians, I will rescue you from their bondage, and I will redeem you with an outstretched arm with great judgements

I may not be living in Egypt but I do have burdens in my life. This is one of those promises that I asked you to hunt for in the Bible. The promise here is that we are told we will be rescued from whatever holds us in bondage. The lesson of the devotional was that when we set out to do something that things may not turn out like we think they might. Sometimes things will get worse before they get better but by keeping God in our lives we are able to do anything. I love knowing I have such awesome support in my life. My plan was to send Chris out into the world and watch him grow and hopefully be successful but God had a different plan. With Gods plan it turned my world upside down and He wanted me to lean on Him to turn it right side up again. I reached for that outstretched arm for all the support I could get.

Day 6: 1 Corinthians 3:13 Each one's work
will become clear; for the Day will declare it,
because it will be revealed by fire; and the fire
will test each one's work, of what sort it is.

It is important that we live our lives with the purpose of serving God. Oh, I'm sure to some of us this sounds to much like hard work but when we put forth the efforts and do this the reward(s) we are blessed with is so wonderful. As I have grown in my walk with the Lord I've become more obedient to His word and I strive to do all things for Him with the purpose of furthering His kingdom. This could be anything from writing this book to just being kind and gentle throughout my day, being that living example of Jesus. I want to do things for Jesus! One day when I stand in front of Jesus I want to stand before Him boldly, not hanging my head in shame. Let me give you a practical example of this way of living. I have a goal to learn how to use my sewing machine so that I can start making pillows. Now I could make pillows and give them away as gifts and or make pillows and sell them to make money. I could decorate my pillows any way I like and make as many as I like and then do with the money anything I like. However, I want to live a life pleasing to God so my choices become a little different. First, I will go to God in prayer and ask for Him to give me the ability to learn how to use my sewing machine. Next, when I decorate my pillows I will do them in a way that will benefit God. I'd probably choose to do this by putting Bible verses on them or something of that sort. Afterward when I have a number of pillows made I could give them away or sell them. Instead of using the money for my desires I would choose to use the money for charity and missions or the food bank. One choice is for self gain and the other is to help further Gods kingdom. I want the hobby but find it much more exciting to learn how to sew when I know what I can do with that hobby for God. I want to live with the purpose of serving God. Find what excites you and ask God to help you how you may use that to serve Him.

> Day 7: Deuteronomy 6:6-7 "And these words which I command you today shall be in your heart. 7) You shall teach them diligently to your children, and shall talk to them when you sit in your house, when you walk by the way, when you lie down, and when you rise up.

If there is anything that I am happy and relived about is knowing that I brought Christopher to church. Christopher excepted Jesus into his heart that night when the teens had their overnighter. Who would of known what would of happened if Red hadn't of taken Chris to that event. What did happen though is Jesus knocked on Chris's door and Chris choose to open it. It gives me a peace within me knowing Chris is part of Gods kingdom. Teaching our children doesn't always have to be a sit down open book Bible study. In fact, I have found them the most challenging with my children. Giggles and rolling of the eyes and starring contests made it difficult. What does work well for me though is just everyday living. With every subject of life is a Bible lesson to go with it. From discipline to showing love for everyone, why not to gossip, how to spend their money, premarital sex, sacrifice, giving, taking and on and on I could go. It's all in there. Learn it and pass it on, you'll be glad you did.

Day 8: Exodus 4:17 You shall take this rod in
your hand, with which you shall do signs.

I almost decided not to put this days devotion in this list of days because it contains the word "signs". People seem to seek out "signs" that God is speaking to them or trying to show them something or directing them a certain way if they get stuck in that thought process of what a sign could be. In this verse the word "sign" is meant to show that Moses had the instrument by which miracles that God would do would be used through this rod. That being said, the daily devotional was teaching us that what little we have God can use it for great purposes. There was nothing little about Chris's life except the amount of time he had it here on earth and God is using that now to serve His purpose. If part of that plan is to grow me as a stronger Christian then I will not push aside these lessons I've been growing in sense Chris has passed. As painful as this experience has been I refuse to let it all be a waste.

Day 9: Romans 12:2 Be transformed
by the renewing of your mind.

This verse here is like a pot of gold when desiring how to become a more dedicated Christian. Filling your mind with Bible scripture allows the Holy Spirit to work in you. When things come up in your life or your acting in an undesirable way put into your mind what would the Bible teach on that. For those of us who don't memorize things to quickly, carry around verses that have meaning to you whether on a flash card or notebook. You can even find smaller sized Bibles in bookstores and you can highlight verses so you can find them quicker. Whatever it takes to keep

Gods word near to you. Don't be so hard on yourself if you make mistakes either. God grows us in steps so don't expect to know everything to soon. The world around you has more influence then you may realize but it can be overcome. Be patience with yourself, God knows your heart and He will be your helper along the way.

During this week before Chris's accident it had already been planted in my heart that I was going to do things God's way when I would need to. As that is how it seemed to me when I believed God was speaking to me. So when that time did come I didn't do everything perfectly and a few times I even reminded myself of the promise I'd made to God. If your hearts desire is to grow then rest assured that God will make it happen.

Day 10: Ephesians 2:14 He Himself is our peace, who has made both one, and has broken down the middle wall of separation.

Without Jesus our world would still live in separation. It used to be Jews and Gentiles. When Jews refused to except Him as the Massiah, Jesus welcomed the Gentiles (all other peoples of the earth) to know Him as Lord and Savior, the son of the living God. Don't feel as if you were rejected and not part of Gods family; God had it all planned out so that all His children would be part of His kingdom. What this shows is that nothing divides Gods children and we are all equal in His eyes.

I had to remind myself at the hospital a couple of times that we are ALL Gods children. God was using this tragic time with Chris for all that were involved. When I had those moments of resentment I'd have to repeat in my head the reminder that we are all Gods children. This shelved those negative thoughts and that is were I've tried to leave them.

Day 11: Amos 4:12 Prepare to meet your God!

Well, didn't this verse just send some shock waves through me when I read it again. With that exclamation point at the end of the verse it seems like a warning of sorts. Like, hello, I'm sending a lightning bolt your way. But it's not. After reading the daily devotion over again it is a reminder that we should get to know our God while we are still here on earth, not to wait until we are face to face with Him. Since He has taken Chris home I have been doing just that. I realize more then ever that our time will come to die off this earth and we just don't know when that will be. Therefore, I want to learn and live as much as I can on how to serve God best. It's not that I want to earn brownie points; it's because knowing Jesus is a personal relationship and I grow to know Him more and more each time I study Gods word. When I meet Jesus face to face He won't be someone unfamiliar to me; I'll just finally know what He looks like.

Neglected Verses

The following three verses are the verses that were in my daily devotion the three days that Chris was in the hospital. Under the circumstances you don't have to imagine why I never got to them. Although, I was distracted with my circumstances God continued to speak to me through the devotional. He was there for me; I wasn't however, mindful of my daily reading. If I had been more aware of taking that time look at how He was speaking to me.

First day of the accident: Colossians 4:6 Let your speech always be with grace, seasoned with salt, that you may know how you ought to answer each one.

This would be the verse that I messed up on. I know for sure that I wasn't speaking well at the hospital in Dover-Foxcroft. I was angry and I did not hide it. Over the next couple of days I had to pray to God about all this and kept reminding myself of the promise I had made to Him.

Second day of the accident: Psalm 131:2 Surely I have calmed and quieted my soul.

This day the devotional is using a partial verse to teach us not to let the noise of the world distract us from being in prayer with God so that we may hear Him when He is speaking to us. I didn't read this devotion but you can know for sure that I was in prayer with God countless times about my circumstance. I have learned long ago how important prayer is and it is only natural for me to keep that line of communication open. I never get a busy signal when I call on God, no matter what time of day or night He is always waiting to hear from me.

Third and final day of the accident: 2 Corinthians 1:3 Blessed be the God and Father of our Lord Jesus Christ, the Father of mercies and God of all comfort.

Again, the daily devotion was teaching on the importance of prayer. With prayer God is able to give us comfort in our trials. If we have inner sorrows that distract us from God He isn't able to offer us His consolation. What a lesson and what timing with that lesson! To bad I didn't read it the day I should of. However, like I've already told you, I was praying so I was allowing God to console me. I am thankful I allowed Him to be with me then and now as I continue on this journey.

This journey has long since passed the official mourning period but my life has had to continue on. My heart still aches at the loss of Chris. I just have to keep moving forward. I've chosen to give this hurt over to our Lord and read His word so that I can have the strength to keep moving on with my life. This life I have I want to use it in a positive manner. I don't want to become stagnant. I continue to take deep breaths and know that God is with me and only wants to grow me. I choose to go to church, I choose to go to Bible study, I choose to read my Bible, I choose to have my daily devotions, I choose to listen only to Christian radio, I choose to pray. Striving always to keep Jesus the focus of my days. Do I always want to choose to do these things. No. I'm human, I get tired and lazy and moody but I don't let those times take my life over. I've chosen Jesus and each day that I'm given I want to grow to be more like Him.

Distractions

As I sit here and type out these words do you have any idea what day it is? Let me not hold you in suspense. This day is Monday, June 10, 2013! Where one's life journey will take them is not always what we have planned. A lesson that I am sure you have gathered from reading this book. I have to shake my head in this dumbfounded way that I am feeling in this moment. Life took me on an entire different course then what I had charted. My plan was to have this book all typed up by winters end, which here in Maine doesn't go by the calender. To me that means when the snow melts so that I can get myself out in the yard doing spring clean-up.

I believe that as much as I am working to get this book completed for God that Satan is at work trying to make sure that it isn't completed. The fear alone about what people might think of this book hasn't been enough to stop me so what makes Satan think I am going to get distracted enough to not finish this work. I'm sure he is going by my track record. Well, hello, my desire is to grow in the Lord and this is one of those times that I am saying "yes" to God; regardless of the gut wrenching butterflies I will cross the finish line. Still, Satan has been relentless right form the beginning of this project.

From day one Satan has tried to put an end to my work for the Lord. The first attempt was having the electricity go out while I was busy typing the introduction to this book. There I was typing away with my mind totally focused on my work that I never realized the electricity went out until across my screen came the warning that my computers battery was about to run out. I flew into a panic trying to get the last few sentences typed. Usually, I take my time and try to get each line just right and then re-read everything as I continue on. Not this time. I typed as fast as I could and left any errors, then tried to remember how to save a new folder. With heart racing and hands starting to sweat I managed with my first attempt to get my pages saved. Ha ha, Satan lost that round.

Santan's second attempt to end my project gave me quite a scare. This time I have to say he went all out. I had been working away one day and then put my computer aside until my daughter came home. I had asked her if she was interested in what I had written and she had said yes. I got my computer and opened my file and read her my days work. I closed down my computer as usual and placed it back on the coffee table. No big deal; just routine stuff. Well, the next day when I went to use my computer it wouldn't do anything. It was just black! For no apparent reason my computer had crashed. I was bewildered! How could this of happened? All I did was turn it on and then shut it off! My husband took it to the computer store to have it checked out. I was freaking out! The big question was were they going to be able to save any of my files! My book! All that work! I didn't want to have to start over! It took five long agenizing weeks to get the final answer to my fears. They were able to save my files! That was a huge release of breath that time. I prayed so hard during that time and besides my husband I only told one other person and she prayed also. It was time to get back to business and I wanted to give it my all because once again we were entering the holiday season. My time was going to become limited once again being shared with Christmas shopping, wrapping gifts, decorating. Just the busyness of the holiday. There was also the "time" I had to consider the children being on Christmas break. That doesn't end until the new year begins. There would be no holding this time back and no holding onto it. Once it came and went, back to work I went. I kept setting myself a new deadline. By the end of February, then that time would pass and I'd set it to the end of March finally I just set it for when the snow passed. It all seemed realistic each time I'd set a new date but then again Satan would be at work trying to interfere with my progress.

Less then three weeks later our youngest son had gotten himself suspended from school. He would be out of school for two days, two days that I wouldn't be able to focus on my work. This was also at the end of the week so I was going to be away from my work four days in a row. Once he returned to school I was able to get myself back to my work and relieved that once more I would have some time to myself. This would give me about three weeks of solid school days to get my work completed. Yes, he had some detentions thrown in the mix but at least I was making progress with my work. I even came to believe that I would reach the end of this project sooner then I thought. Oh, but wait we are discussing Satan here, the one with countless tricks up his sleeve. Once again, there would come yet another phone call from school explaining how our youngest son was suspended again. This time it was even more serious of an offense. This time required him to be out of school six days! I wasn't pleased but started to see the situation for what it was. Another distraction, another circumstance attempting to draw me away from the one thing I want to get done and doing it for God.

Next came another shocker, one that put a screeching halt to all my progress on this book. I had been working away when the phone rang. Another phone call from the school. This conversation involved the question whether or not our youngest son was going to be able to return to school or not. We were given three options. One, our youngest son could stop going to school and continue back in the fall still as a tenth grader. Two, he could be transferred to another school or third, he could go before the board and face a possible explosion. I was given time to talk this matter over with my husband and let them know what the decision was at the beginning of the coming week. This allotted time also gave me plenty of opportunity to go before our Lord in prayer. I needed that time. I was once again in my life trying to fight back feelings of resentment. I was able to get past the "poor me" pity party on how all this was going to effect my life and do what I thought it was that God would have me do. I prayed on this and was given a peace about what the final outcome was to be. I didn't chose any of the three given choices. Instead, when I called the school and spoke with the headmaster I offered a fourth solution which was accepted. This solution was to pull our youngest son out of school and with the assistance of his teachers let me home-school him for the remainder of the year. With only two and one half months of this I thought it possible to manage and thought it best for our son. So to work with school business I went. It turned out that once our youngest son set his mind to getting his school work accomplished that is took less time to complete then originally intended. His last day of school was April 30th.

What happened to the month of May you might ask? Well, guilty as charged. May arrived and so did the warmer temperatures. Outside became very inviting and I was drawn into the warmth of the sunshine. Being I was done being a school teacher I thought I needed to keep our youngest son busy during the day. I didn't want him to think it was time to be on vacation when everyone else still had to get up and take care of their responsibilities this time of year. For about two and a half weeks I did every chore I could find to do. We picked up sticks, picked rocks for the stonewall, picked rocks for the driveway bank, cleaned the goat stall and pen, cleared sand away from the roadside, raked leaves, pulled weeds and lastly rid our wild cherry trees of gypsy-moss. That's when my way of doing things came to an ending.

My last chore was taking them yucky leaf eating pest out of our cherry trees. I had decided to take a break form my inside chores and stroll out to see how our youngest sons progress was going with the removal of our goat stall winter bedding. That is when I discovered two nests of gypsy-moss on some eye level tree branches. My grandfather would remove these type of nests with a stick and a coffee can with gas inside so I decided to do the same before they would overtake my yard. Off to work I went and took this chore to the back of our property. I walked around for quite some time removing a fair share of this pest. I had noted the ones out of reach and after getting all I could called our youngest son to grab the ladder and come up to the back. We did a great job together until our last tree. This tree was actually the first tree we did but on our way out I noticed four nests we somehow missed. We propped up the ladder and up went our youngest son. He was able to reach two of the four with the ladder and stepped up on the branch to reach the other two. That is when he stepped and leaned forward only to hear a crack of the tree branch. I had had my back to him but when I heard the crack of the branch turned to look at him in time to see him come crashing about ten feet to the ground. My first thought was hoping that a branch didn't poke him in the eye. They didn't and I figured as usual he would get up and we'd just continue on. Not so. "Oh, I broke my arm", he gasped as he stood up. I looked at his arm and found his left wrist in the form of an "s". I lifted him with his right arm around my neck and asked him please just don't pass out on me. Needless to say, we spent the next few hours at our local hospital in the ER.

The broken wrist just wasn't a simple fix. As it turned out he was given a splint and some pain medicine with instructions to go to Bangor the next morning. The wrist was shattered to a point of needing surgery which at that time four pins were planted in his arm. At this time we are now in the healing process.

Since that Friday afternoon there has been countless days of rain. Instead of wrapping my mind around getting back into my book I've been admittedly lazy. I've excused myself from working on this book in many fashionable ways. First, I've wanted to allow my body to get past the aches and pains of the yard work, then I had to keep up with the reading I want to do for Sunday school and Bible study. Other days I would go back to bed being it was a rainy day anyway. On and on with nothing but excuses. Until this past week when I started getting the desire back in my heart that this book really needs to get completed. Bottom line was that I was allowing Satan to get his way with me after all. That is just not going to happen; so here I am proving once again that I am human and I am picking myself up and "brushing off the dust" and moving forward. I will not give up!

Our youngest son hasn't been the only distraction come my way these past months. One of my favorite distractions is when the telephone rings. That one just makes me laugh because I fall for it every time. If I know who is calling me then I find it difficult to pretend I'm not here. Besides, what if they were in need of something serious? I've also had a sinus infection and stomach viruses. When I was really getting this book pumped out I developed a very uncomfortable ache in my right thumb joint but chose to ignore that one. I would also have my dog start barking for no apparent reason while trying to concentrate on my work. There is also the cat getting in on this too. I've never had a cat that wouldn't settle down for the night. Our cat loves to jump on my bed and disrupt my sleep to a point that I'm still tired in the morning. Closing my bedroom door sounds like the obvious answer to this problem but our cat is to clever for that. He reaches up with his paw and jiggles the doorknob until you let him in or out of the door. It was cute when he wanted to go outside but after he learned he could do this with my bedroom doorknob I was defeated. I now leave the door opened a bit so that he can come and go on his choosing without waking me or my husband up with the sound of the jiggle. He leaves my husband alone but still disrupts my sleep by tiptoeing around me and if that doesn't wake me he will nibble on my fingernails. I don't have the heart to put him outside at night with all the wildlife so that isn't even an option.

Whatever the distraction this book will get completed. It may not be in my timing but it will be in Gods timing. Like anything in this world, if it is Gods will then His will will be done. It gives me comfort knowing I'm on the winning team.

Farewell My Friend

I t is difficult for me in this moment. It is a time that is bitter sweet. I've looked forward to having this book completed so that you could hold it in your hands and possibly have it change your heart. Although, having to close this out means not having you here to "talk" to.

I've let you enter into a small portion of my life to reveal to you that even being a Christian isn't always easy. We all have our ups and downs; the trials that come our way. We all live and grow and change and develop different attitudes. We go through fazes and fads and discover things about ourselves along the way. Our difference is who are we letting lead us. Are you independent and can handle the world on your own? Or are you letting the world lead you in your decision making? Or are you letting God lead you? God sent us His son, Jesus, and that is who a Christian follows. We do our best to live the example Jesus set for us. Though we are not perfect, we don't give up the race we are in and we know our destination.

There's only one thing in this life that is for certain. That certainty, is that we all will die. I don't believe that you aren't aware of this fact and if you aren't then I am sorry that I am the one that has opened your eyes to this information. It doesn't have to be all doom and glume. As a Christian, we believe that once we are gone from this earth that our life continues on with our Lord. That we will be with Him in His heavenly kingdom. We believe that our spirit leaves our fleshly body and continues on. We are here on earth for an appointed time and then we go to be with our Lord. That is part of the joy a Christian has; knowing our destination.

As with our friend, Jason Ham, I can not leave you wondering if you know this Jesus I speak about. I knew I would be moving away from Springfield, ME and ran to Jason's car to get my answer.

I am so glad that I don't have that on my mind anymore. It is the same for me now. I want to reach out to ask you the same question. Will you be living in Gods kingdom? If I never meet you here will I meet you there? Are you having that tug at your heart and want to give into it but fear and/or doubt may be holding you back? Have you tried everything is your life but still have that knocking at the door? Tell me, please, what is holding you back?

I or anyone else in this world cannot make this decision for you. God Himself will not force Himself for you to answer His call. It's your choice. I know what I would have you do. Just as I wanted for Christopher and all our children. But when I think of Christopher, my question to you isn't just a question anymore. It's a plea. It's a plea because I have come to know how things can change in an instance.

My eyes are brimming with tears that are soon to spill over onto my cheeks. The tears come because I miss our Christopher. I know his life here was short and I want you to realize that not one of us knows when our time here is to come to an end. That's okay though, when you know your destination is heavenward. I just know how much God loves you and wants you to be there too.

Before I leave you I just have one more question. Would you just take a short walk with me? It just may change the rest of your life.

Walk This Way

This walk I want to take you on is called the Roman Road. This is the point where you can make the choice whether you want to go down this road now or not Or it may be something you want to come back to later. For those of you that have decided to take this walk let me tell you what this is going to do for you.

Taking this walk is going to lead you into a life with Jesus. The Bible uses verses from the book of Romans to guide you along the way of giving your life over to Christ. Which simply means that you are going to live your life the best you can by letting Him lead you. You are going to learn how to let Him do this by studying the Bible and learning how Jesus handled His life here on earth. Jesus is going to reveal Himself to you and He is also going to reveal you to yourself. Things are not always going to be comfortable but when you know that it is to benefit your spiritual growth these uncomfortable changes become welcome changes. You'll even grow to a point where you welcome and desire these changes. You'll grow to a place where you want to be obedient to Gods word and you'll find yourself making changes in your life with things you thought you could never live without. It's all quite exciting and can be a refreshing challenge. In the end of all ends when we all enter Gods kingdom FOREVER I do not for a moment doubt that this is a choice that you'll be glad you made. Come on now, it's only a few short steps.

I am going to include the Bible verses out of the New King James version of the Bible for those of you that may not have a Bible with you in this moment. First though, please know that God loves you!

John 3:16 For God so loved the world that He gave His only begotten Son,

that whoever believes in Him should not perish but have everlasting life.

This verse tells us that God loves us and Jesus is Gods Son whom He sent to save us so that we may be with Him forever. Anyone who calls out to Jesus will be saved. Are you ready?

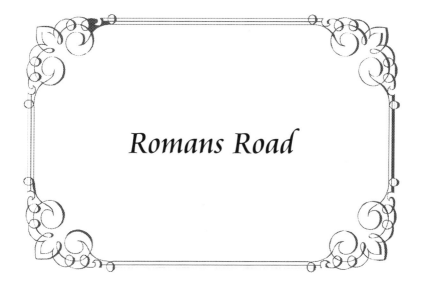

Romans Road

omans 3:23 for all have sinned and fall short of the glory of God

Our sins have kept us separated from God. Remember, we are all sinners and no one person is any better then another. In Gods eye, sin is sin. Jesus takes that separation away by dying on the cross for our sins. Jesus took our punishment so that we may be reunited with God. We can only get to God through Jesus. When we choose to turn back to God through Jesus we will be blessed with the gift of everlasting life in Gods kingdom.

Romans 6:23 For the wages of sin is death, but the gift of God is eternal life in Christ Jesus our Lord.

Our payment for the choice of continuing to walk in sin is death; a separation from God forever in hell. To choose to walk away from sin and choose Jesus is a free gift given by God to all of us that are undeserving.

Romans 5:8 But God demonstrates His own love toward us, in that while we were still sinners, Christ died for us.

You are Gods creation and He loves you unconditionally. Jesus left HEAVEN to come to this earth to fulfill the will of God. Jesus did that when He gave Himself up to a punishment that was ours and rose again to go back to heaven.

Romans 10:13 "For whoever calls on the name of the Lord shall be saved."

Now it's your turn. Are you ready? Call on the name of Jesus and ask Him into your heart and your life and let Him be your Lord and Savior. Just talk to Him (prayer) and admit to Him that if you were to die today that you wouldn't be going to heaven. Tell him you know you are a sinner and confess those sins to Him. Ask Him for forgiveness of these sins and ask Him to come into your life to be your Lord and Savior. Ask Him for His help in living a life for Him from this day forward. Then lastly, thank Him for saving you by dying on the cross. Thank Him for anything you want and pray all these things in Jesus name.

Congratulations! Your name has just been written in the Book of Life! The angels are rejoicing and I am rejoicing! I am so happy that your everlasting life has just begun!

Now come here, my friend, let me hug you long and hard. I have to go now but rest assured we will one day meet again. By the way, if you get there before me can you tell Chris I said hello and I miss him so.

And do not be conformed to this world;
but be transformed by the renewing of your mind,
that you may prove what is that good and
acceptable and perfect will of God.

Romans 12:2

Printed in the United States
By Bookmasters